Bobby Jones
GOLF TIPS

Edited by
Sidney L. Matthew

CITADEL PRESS

Kensington Publishing Corp.

www.kensingtonbooks.com

CITADEL PRESS BOOKS are published by

Kensington Publishing Corp.
850 Third Avenue
New York, NY 10022

Copyright © 1999 Sidney L. Matthew

Previously published as a hardcover by Sleeping Bear Press

All Kensington titles, imprints, and distributed lines are available at special quantity discounts for bulk purchases for sales promotions, premiums, fund-raising, educational, or institutional use. Special book excerpts or customized printings can also be created to fit specific needs. For details, write or phone the office of the Kensington special sales manager: Kensington Publishing Corp., 850 Third Avenue, New York, NY 10022, attn: Special Sales Department, phone 1-800-221-2647.

CITADEL PRESS and the Citadel logo are Reg. U.S. Pat. & TM Off.

Sketches by Ed Lloyd

First printing: May 2004

10   9   8   7   6   5   4   3   2   1

Printed in the United States of America

Library of Congress CIP Data on File

ISBN 0-8065-2621-1

ACKNOWLEDGMENTS

During the zenith of his golfing career, Bob Jones wrote bi-weekly golf columns for the Bell Syndicate from 1927 until 1935 under the bylines "Bobby Jones Says," "My Theories of Golf" and "Bobby Jones on Golf." A selection of these articles was included in *Bobby Jones on Golf* first published in 1929 by One Time Productions, Inc., copyright 1931 by Bell Syndicate, Inc. Excerpts were revised in 1997 by Sidney L. Matthew, published in *Bobby Jones on Golf* by Sleeping Bear Press and in *Secrets of the Master: The Best of Bobby Jones* published in 1996, edited by Sidney L. Matthew and published by Sleeping Bear Press. The excerpts published herein are included in the original writings originally published by the Bell Syndicate.

TABLE OF CONTENTS

FOREWORD

"Friendship"

In 1958, my grandfather, Robert Tyre Jones, Junior, traveled to St. Andrews, Scotland, for the inaugural World Amateur Team Championships at the Old Course. Bub (a family nickname) had been asked by the United States Golf Association to captain the American team. Although he had not held a golf club for more than a decade and was feeling the painful effects of the neurological disease condition that would eventually rob him of his physical freedom, he decided to go to Saint Andrews, the site of his greatest failure and his greatest triumphs.

Bub first set eyes on the Old Course in the 1921 British Open. He was a cocky 19-year-old, with a reputation for prodigious skill and fiery temper, and did not appreciate either the tradition or the subtlety of the Old Course. Although he had played fairly well in the first two rounds, in the third round he hacked his way to a 46 on the first nine holes. He came to the eleventh hole, a short par three, disgusted with himself and with the course. His tee shot on eleven landed in the Hill Bunker, and after three or four attempts, he pocketed the ball and tore up his scorecard, withdrawing from the Open Championship. The British press was merciless in their criticism of him. One daily even wrote, "Bobby Jones is a boy, and an ordinary boy at that." Bub was stung by the criticism, and decided that he would never again allow his emotions to defeat him on the golf course. He also determined that he would study and come to appreciate the Old Course of St. Andrews. His study of the Old Course paid great dividends as he went undefeated in the Walker Cup matches in 1926, and won the British Open there in 1927. His final victory on the Old Course came in the British Amateur of 1930, the first leg of the Grand Slam.

In addition to a respect for the Old Course, Bub also earned the love of the people of St. Andrews. In 1936, while visiting Scotland, he decided to return to the Old Course for a friendly round of golf. He had hoped to keep the visit quiet, but the word spread quickly around the town. Shopkeepers closed their businesses for the day, hanging signs in their windows that said, simply, "Bobby's Back!" Schoolchildren left their classrooms, housewives abandoned their chores, and the people of the Royal Burgh of St. Andrews gathered on their Old Course to join their Bobby on his return. It was one of the most emotional experiences of his life, and it cemented a bond between the city and him that lasted to his dying day.

When he arrived at St. Andrews in 1958, he was informed that the city had decided to confer upon him the honor of "Freeman of St. Andrews." Although he was touched by the sincerity of the gesture, he did not consider it to be much more than receiving a "key to the city." However, as he learned more about the honor, he realized that the significance of the "Freedom" was far greater than he had first thought, or even could imagine. To be a "Freeman of St. Andrews" was to be adopted by these people and this town. To be a "Freeman" was to become one with the people of St. Andrews, it was an act of intimacy and generosity that was bestowed by the people only on those with whom they felt a closeness in spirit. So, on October 9, 1958, the people of St. Andrews packed Younger Hall at the University. With an overflow crowd, Bub was presented the honor of the Freedom, one of only a few to receive this dignity, and only the second American, the first being Benjamin Franklin in 1759.

The crowd hushed as he approached the dais to receive the silver casket containing the scroll that declared his new status. He had prepared remarks for the event, but the papers never left his pocket. He recounted in his book, *Golf Is My Game*, his words of that night. This is some of what he said:

"Friends are a man's priceless treasures, and a life rich in friendship is full indeed.

"When I say, with due regard for the meaning of the word, that I am your friend, I have pledged to you the ultimate in loyalty and devotion. In some respects friendship may even transcend love, because in friendship there is no place for jealousy. When I say, without more, that you are my friends, it is possible that I may be imposing upon you a greater burden than you are willing to assume. But when you have made me aware on many occasions that you have a kindly feeling toward me, and when you have honored me by every means at your command, then when I call you my friend, I am at once affirming my high regard and affection for you and declaring my complete faith in you and trust in the sincerity of your expressions. And, so my fellow citizens of St. Andrews, it is with this appreciation of the full sense of the word that I salute you as my friends."

These words have always struck me as being highly significant, but I first came to really appreciate the significance of them almost 20 years later, and the person who embodied these ideals more than anyone I have ever known was Joseph C. Dey.

Mr. Dey, as I always called him, was, among other things, the former Executive Director of the United States Golf Association, the first Commissioner of the PGA Tour, and a former Captain of the Royal and Ancient Golf Club of St. Andrews. During his life, he held virtually every position of honor in golf that one could hold. Yet for all his honors, he was a man of great modesty, and gentle civility. Charlie Yates, 1938

British Amateur champion, has frequently said of my grandfather, "A man never stands so tall as when he stoops to help a boy." There are several people in my life who have filled this mold. Few people will ever stand taller in my eyes than Mr. Dey, and this is why.

I attended my first Masters in 1970 at the age of 12 years. I had little interest in golf at that time, but I looked forward to being there for the tournament. My father served on the Rules Committee that year, and I remember times in the evening when we would look out over the course and he would explain the intricacies of the Augusta National layout, explaining why Bub designed certain holes the way he did. He also told me other stories.

He told me of how my great-grandfather, Robert Purmedus Jones, "Colonel Bob" to his friends, would sing "Old Man River" in the shower in the upstairs locker room. The Colonel would sing with such gusto that it could be heard all the way down at the twelfth green, a substantial distance away. Dad told me about staying in the Jones cabin with the Colonel and Bub. He said that he would start every night sleeping in Bub's room, but sometime during the evening he would have to go to the living room in the middle of the cabin to escape Bub's snoring. There was no respite to be found there, however, because once settled in the living room, my dad was serenaded by both Bub's and the Colonel's snores!

For me, Augusta National became associated with memories of my father and it remains to this day a powerful connection to my father, grandfather, and even the great-grandfather who died before I was born. When my father died unexpectedly in December 1973, I stopped going to the Masters for several years.

When I finally returned several years later, it was a difficult experience. Everywhere I went I was reminded of my father. I made it through Thursday and Friday, but on Saturday morning, I arrived at the Club early in the morning. I was so despondent that I called my mother in Nashville and told her that I was coming home that morning. She said, "Son, I know it's tough. But just go to the clubhouse, have some breakfast, and then see how you feel. If you still want to come home in the afternoon, then that will be O.K."

I took Mom's advice and found a table in the clubhouse and sat down to breakfast. I had just sipped my orange juice when I heard a voice behind me say, "Good morning, Bob. May I join you for breakfast?" I looked up to see Mr. Dey looking down at me with a gentle smile on his face. He sat down to eat and we spent the next 45 minutes talking about the tournament and golf. Before he left, he asked if he could join me for breakfast the next morning and we made arrangements to meet at eight. My spirits were brighter after that and I enjoyed the day. More importantly, I didn't go home.

The next morning, I arrived at the clubhouse at eight, found a table, and sat down to wait for Mr. Dey. At eight-fifteen he still hadn't arrived and my spirits were rapidly taking a southerly turn. I tried to rationalize that a person of Mr. Dey's importance probably was tied up with another equally important person in the golf world. Or, worse, that maybe he had just forgotten that he's made breakfast arrangements with me. I was sinking fast into the morass of self-pity when I saw him come through the door. He came straight to the table. He was slightly breathless when he said, "I'm so sorry to be late. I was tied up in traffic coming back from church. I try to start my Sunday mornings with Holy Communion and I was at church. It makes my week so much easier." Then he relaxed. "Have you seen the pairings for the day?" And we were talking about the sport that had brought us both together: Golf.

I don't know if Mr. Dey ever knew what he did for me that weekend. He transformed Augusta National for me. Prior to those two days, Augusta had become the tomb of my memories for my father and grandfather. Following that weekend, it was a place of fellowship, where people gathered to celebrate the Royal and Ancient Game.

I have been blessed in my life to know some remarkable

men. Charlie Yates is one and I owe him more than I will ever be able to repay. Another great man who has been formative in my life is Walter Wattles, an insurance executive in Atlanta. But on an April weekend, when I was feeling the loss of my Dad, Joe Dey stood larger than life, transformed my pain into pleasant memories, and gave me new memories to build on. I will always be grateful.

*   *   *

There are friends and there are friends. Some friends are casual and, when the going gets rough, may be hard to find. Others, when times are tough, get down in the trench with you, put their backs to yours, and help you fight the fight. Sid Matthew is one of the latter category of friends. I am honored to write these words for this volume, and I thank Sidney Matthew for all of his efforts to make my grandfather live to a new generation of golfers.

Robert Tyre Jones IV

INTRODUCTION

While reading Bob Jones' golf tips contained in this volume, I was again reminded what a great player Jones actually was and the wonderful gift Jones had for expressing himself. Jones was a special person. He was modest enough that he never sought a comparison of his own golfing greatness to others in the history of the game. But it seems to me that the reader must know something about how Jones stacks up in golf history to appreciate how important his thoughts on the game really are.

As I near the age when fans are beginning to regard me as a sort of elder statesman of golf, I find that I am expected to sit on a bench by a tee and discuss the old and the new with frank informality. As the only professional who played with the old-timers of the Vardon era and who continues to match shots, or tries to, with the 4-H Club—Harbert, Harrison, Heafner, and Hamilton—and the other leaders of the pack, I am constantly being asked about the relative merits of golfers who reached their peaks in different decades: How would Jones have come out against Hogan? Would Nelson have been able to stand up to Hagen in match play and trim him in medal? How well would Snead have scored in the 1920s, when the rough was rougher, the greens unwatered, the steel-shaft undeveloped, the sand-iron uninvented, and totals in the 260s unimaginable?

Most of the time I have a fairly good idea of the answer my inquisitor is seeking. If he is older than I am, he generally wants affirmation that the newer styles would have been far less devastating in the earlier decades when golf was, admittedly, a much harder game than it is today. On the other hand, the persons who are younger than I am want to hear that Hogan would have easily out-Jonesed Jones, out-Vardoned Vardon, and out-Morrised young Tom Morris had he competed in their respective eras. They're tough, these queries, and it's hard to give an objective answer. While I do not consciously try to be diplomatic and appease the worshippers of the various heroes, I honestly do not know who would have beaten whom—the Hagen of 1924, the Jones of 1930, the Nelson of 1945, or the Hogan of 1948. It would have depended, probably, on what day it was.

The more I think of the comparative qualities of the masters who have flourished over the past thirty years—or since golf entered its modern phase following World War I—the more I am convinced that for me, anyhow, there must be two major considerations in any rating of golfers: What major championships did the man win? Over how long a period was he a winner?

I know that this last is somewhat unfair to Ben Hogan, whose career was first interrupted by the war and then halted by that awful accident when Ben was in his prime. I know that the first consideration works against Byron Nelson, who reached his peak at a time when major championships were suspended because of the war. As I am continually reminded by the devotees of Mac Smith, Harry Cooper, Horton Smith, and Jimmy Demaret in particular, the emphasis I feel should be placed on major victories does not give the benefit of the doubt to some of our most skillful shotmakers who, for one reason or another, could never break through in national championships. I respect the late Mac Smith, for example, as one of the game's most accomplished artists, an almost classic swinger, but I cannot rate him as high as the champions. It would be unfair to those who succeeded in winning. They had to have an extra something to win. I have lost enough to be tremendously sympathetic toward the runner-up. I have won enough to appreciate how terribly hard it is to win.

As I see it, in the period from 1919 through 1949—I cannot rate Vardon, who belongs to an earlier era—there have been two golfers in a class by themselves: Bob Jones and Walter Hagen.

Jones was great because he had the finest mind of any competitive golfer. He was a brilliant student in college and was an extremely able lawyer and businessman. Jones had a natural genius for hitting a golf ball—he went to the third round of the Amateur at the age of fourteen—but there have been other youngsters with approximate if not equal aptitudes whose names do not appear on the championship cups. Robert T. Jones, Jr. is emblazoned on all the major trophies—once on the British Amateur, three times on the British Open, four times on the United States Open, and five times on the United States Amateur—because he had, along with a great golf game and great fortitude, great intelligence. Jones was able to master his temper and every other problem that stood between him and consistent superlative performance. He knew exactly what he wanted to do. He set his sights on the four major championships each year. When he accomplished his incredible Grand Slam in 1930, Jones retired from competition.

Jones' long, rhythmical, truly spectacular swing was not the type of swing that could have stood up to continuous tournament stress. I think that if it had been necessary for Jones to play week-in and week-out tournament golf, he would have had to make some changes in his swing, and there is no doubt that Jones could have done so as successfully as Ezio Pinza switched from the less intensive schedule of opera to the grind of musical comedy. As it was, Jones' swing had a bravura quality to it. It took quite a bit of time to tune it delicately to tournament pitch, and it took a great deal of care to keep it on pitch. Near the end of Jones' career I thought I noticed that he had to keep watch against his swing's becoming too flat. It seemed to me that he exaggerated the pronation of his right wrist when he addressed the ball, as if he were consciously trying to open his clubhead a trifle. Jones' irons were better than good, but it was his driving and his putting that always impressed me most. He was remarkably straight off the tee in all kinds of weather and under all kinds of pressure, and when he wanted distance he could be as long as any of the boys. I don't think the present generation has any idea of how wonderful Jones was on the greens. His lovely smooth stroke on his long approach putts left him with little kick-ins time after time. He had a superb sense of distance.

Jones was a fine man to be partnered with in a tournament. Congenial and considerate, he made you feel that you were playing with a friend, and you were. At the same time, in a unique and wondrous way, Jones quietly unleashed the most furious concentration of any golfer, in those days when it was Jones versus the field. This arduous dedication to the job at hand left him spent and weary after each round. Jones never hung around the locker room long after his day's play was over. Hagen—you could never get him out. The two great champions were completely dissimilar in their attitudes toward crowds. Jones was always polite toward his idolatrous galleries, but I think he regarded them as an element that could deter his concentration if he let it invade his thoughts. Hagen loved the crowd. He hated to have to leave his gallery at the conclusion of a match, and did everything he could to postpone that painful parting. In their one man-against-man meeting in Florida in 1926, Walter administered a decisive lacing to Bob, but it is notable that Walter never was able to win an Open Championship in which Jones was entered. Walter had Jonesitis as bad as the rest of us.

I know that these golf tips written by Jones himself will help your understanding of what you are trying to do and how you are trying to do it. I'll be sure to tell Bob when I see him that you and other golfers are still enjoying his timeless tips.

Gene Sarazen

List of Terms

brassie: a wooden club with a brass soleplate designed to protect the club from fracture when a stroke is played from a road or other hard surface; more lofted than the driver.

cleek: an iron-headed club used for driving, and sometimes for putting.

cuppie lie: a ball lying in a shallow hollow such as may have been made by some earlier player having cut out a piece of turf.

long iron: an iron club with little loft designed to drive the ball long distances with a low trajectory and much roll; it has the longest shaft of all iron clubs but not longer than a driver.

mashie: a moderately lofted iron club shorter in the blade than a mid-iron; it is approximately the loft of a modern number five iron.

more lofted club: a club whose face has more angulation and is designed to drive the ball on a higher trajectory, resulting in less roll when the ball strikes the green.

niblick: a club used for bunkers, hazards, and high lofted strokes; the head is small and round, with a great deal of loft; roughly equivalent to a modern number nine iron.

spade shot: a lofted stroke causing the ball to spin and stop without roll; the club has the loft of a modern seven iron.

spoon: a wooden club with a more lofted face than a straight-faced driver; the spoon strikes between the ball and the ground, causing backspin on the ball, which stops on the green without roll.

stymie: the position of adversaries' golf balls wherein the opponent's ball lies directly in the intended line of play of the other player's ball in relation to the hole.

MY THEORIES OF GOLF

In this and the succeeding articles under this title, I am going to set out in an ordered sequence my conception of the proper way to play the various shots in golf. In some respects it will be a recapitulation of many things which I have written from time to time when the ideas and the possible need for giving expression to them have occurred to me.

I am calling these things "My Theories of Golf." Sometimes they can be more than theories. There are certain actions in the golf swing which can be definitely identified and accepted as invariable because they occur in the swings of all first-class players. But there are others which are more or less obscure and which have defied even high-speed photography. In every case I am going to try to describe the swing from the standpoint of sense and feel, rather than from that of the observer or analyst, because it must be in this way that the golfer keeps track of his own actions.

To Describe How He Controls Own Shots.

The intended exposition is therefore to be more of how I go about controlling my own shots as I make them than of what I observe in others or in camera studies of myself. After all, it is more important to know what one should try to do in order to make a good shot than to know what one actually does.

> The difference is not far removed from
> that which I find between myself, as a
> dub billiard player, and a true expert.

There is perhaps no game which encourages theorizing and experimentation so much as golf. A golfer is nearly always eager to try out any new idea which may be suggested or which may occur to him. But, in most cases, the experimenting is done without the background of a basically sound understanding of the mechanics of the swing. The inclination is too strong to regard the new idea with suspicion, and if it does not begin to function at once, to discard it in favor of the old way. It is always easier to fall back into the old habits, however bad they may be, than to keep hammering away at something new, even though it is sound.

Good Golfer Understands Fundamentals.

A certain amount of tuning and experimenting must be continually practiced in order to keep the best swing working successfully. No one has yet acquired the ability to reproduce indefinitely a perfect stroke. But the expert player applies the corrective measures which are needed from time to time upon a broad understanding of fundamentals. He knows the end to which he is working and, therefore, the means which he selects to take him there never are likely to be far out of line.

There is no possibility that a person will have immediate success applying any suggestion which I or anyone else might make. The pupil always expects instant improvement and will not practice patiently when the advice fails to transform him by magic into a successful player. The common tendency, I think, is to discard the suggested alteration after three or four bad holes.

Pupil Must Patiently Cooperate.

The only instruction which can be of any great value is of an educational nature. The pupil must have patience and he must cooperate. He should do his best, working with his instructor, to acquire a sound understanding of the swing as a whole. Not only is this the only way in which his game will improve, but it is the only way in which he can ever become capable of making for himself the little day-to-day adjustments which everyone must make.

In this series, I am going to have only one thing to accomplish—to build up a picture of the complete golf swing in as simple a way as possible, and I hope to do this by starting with the simplest strokes, proceeding from that point to add a little each time, until we arrive at the end. I am aiming at a broad understanding of the whole swing, rather than attempting to cure individual faults. I want to describe how to do the whole thing correctly rather than how to avoid doing a part of it wrong.

Will Start with Putt.

Because the shorter shots involve a less complicated method, a start will be made with the putting. I remember the story, whether true or not, of the man who learned to play golf by first learning to hole a two-foot putt, gradually increasing his length from there. This appeals to me as the logical, sensible order.

ON THE PRINCIPLES AND THEORY OF GOOD PUTTING

There is no part of golf which carries as much uncertainty as the part which is played on the putting green. It has probably been the chief worry of almost everyone who has played the game to develop a method and to encourage a mental attitude which will make for consistently good putting, but somehow form continues to vary here more than in any other department, so that the reliable putter is a rarity even among the most expert golfers.

> There is a thing we call "touch" which controls the length of the putt, and in order to have a good touch a player must be able to judge the speed of the green and the effect of a slope at a glance, and then his stroke must be so delicately adjusted that he can strike the ball a blow of exactly the right strength.

A great many factors have their part in putting. There is a thing we call "touch" which controls the length of the putt, and in order to have a good touch a player must be able to judge the speed of the green and the effect of a slope at a glance, and then his stroke must be so delicately adjusted that he can strike the ball a blow of exactly the right strength. And then, related to these factors, is the selection of the proper line to the hole—a line which will be altered for variations in the speed of the ball.

We are inclined to accept all these things as they come from day to day. These elusive qualities which are the requirements of good putting have defied all our efforts to control them. We all recognize that on some days our judgment of speed and strength is good and we can readily pick out the proper line to the hole. On such days we putt well, but on other days we are continually struggling to lay the long putts at the holeside and the short ones appear to be almost impossible to hole. We console ourselves by saying that putting is in great part confidence, but that is in reality an admission of our helplessness because we know that we cannot expect to have confidence when we are not putting successfully.

We speak of putting as a game of confidence, I think, because on those days when we are able to see the line to the hole and when our judgment of speed is good, we have no particular worry about the result. It is then a simple matter of striking the ball along the selected line. Our confidence that the line chosen is the correct one and that the strength of the putt will not be far off, leaves us free, without any severe effort, to concentrate on striking the ball truly. On those days when the line to the hole is not so clear and we have not the same confidence in our ability to strike the putt with the proper strength, we continue to worry about these things while we are making the stroke.

Certainly I lay no claim to having reduced the art of putting to anything approaching a science in which there is no variation from day to day, but I have found my average on the putting green to be greatly improved by following a few principles, none of which has to do with form or the details of the stroke. The first one is to resist the inclination to look up to the hole while in the act of striking the ball, an inclination which becomes stronger when one's putting becomes uncertain. Different players have devised for themselves different ways of guarding against this tendency. It makes little difference how long the head is kept down so long as one makes certain that the ball has actually been struck before the eye leaves it.

Certainly I lay no claim to having reduced the art of putting to anything approaching a science in which there is no variation from day to day, but I have found my average on the putting green to be greatly improved by following a few principles, none of which has to do with form or the details of the stroke.

Absolute concentration upon the ball is materially aided by substituting for the objective of the putt, instead of the hole itself, a spot on the green somewhere along the intended line. For a putt of six to ten or twelve feet—of the length which one would normally, at least, hope to hole—the spot selected should be about halfway to the hole, and for a putt of more than this length the spot should be no more than fifteen feet from the ball. It should then be the player's aim to strike the ball so that it will roll directly over this spot, and he should forget the hole entirely except insofar as his mental picture of the length of the putt will affect the strength of his blow. In order to become more consistent the player should make up his mind to concentrate every effort on striking the ball truly. If he does this he cannot go very far wrong.

On Confidence in
Short Putts

I always find myself more than a little annoyed—and I have heard many other competitors express the same feeling—when a missed putt of three, four, or five feet is greeted by "Ohs" and "Ahs" and loud guffaws from the gallery. I am sure that many another struggling contestant has, as I have, wished devoutly for an opportunity to watch the author or authors of the loud noise attempt the same job under the same circumstances. I am certain that he or they should find that many short putts, when viewed from a competitious angle, assume a far different aspect than when seen from the outer reaches of the crowd by a person only mildly interest in the result. It is hard to appreciate how many rolls and tiny yet important undulations can be contained in a little over a yard of putting surface, and it is surprising from this distance how slight an error in either direction of speed may cause the putt to stay out.

Missed Putt May Undermine.

But even granted a just appreciation of the physical difficulties of the stroke, the mental or psychological burden completely escapes all but the man who has himself been through it all. To everyone else it is just one stroke—a question merely of a four or five or a win or a half on one hole. If

8

a man has never been there himself, how can he know what the competitor knows—that a loss of confidence in his ability to hole the short putts may ultimately and in logical progression undermine his entire game. He has had it happen before, and I think it is safe to say that he dreads nothing more than this catastrophe, for when it happens there is nothing to be done.

> If a man has never been there himself, how can he know what the competitor knows—that a loss of confidence in his ability to hole the short putts may ultimately and in logical progression undermine his entire game.

The thing works out about this way: The player first leaves himself three to five feet wide of the hole on his approach putt; possibly on the first occasion he has run that much past the hole, an easy thing to do on keen, slippery, putting greens. He misses the putt back. On the next green he softens his stroke a bit too much, leaves the putt short of the hole and misses that. From that point on anything may happen. The player feels that he cannot hole a short putt, he tries too hard to lay the long ones absolutely dead, and he loses his touch altogether.

The next hope is in the second shot, for he feels that he must play all iron shots to within fifteen or twenty feet of the hole in order to be certain of holing out in two putts, and he knows that if he misses the green there is no chance for a recovery or chip and one putt. In this state it is not hard to see how far the ill effect may extend, especially when tense nerves contribute their bit.

A Bit of Putting Advice.

Someone told me a story about an experienced professional who regained his putting confidence by rather drastic means in the middle of a round. Playing well otherwise, he suddenly lost all ability to hole a short putt. After missing several, he was at one hole left with a mean one of about four feet. This time he walked quickly up to the ball, closed his eyes and rapped the recalcitrant sphere straight into the middle of the cup. He holed the next one or two in the normal way and thereafter pursued his way rejoicing.

I should neither dare to attempt nor recommend for others the method employed here, but there can be no question that anxiety and too much cure cause most short putts to go astray. When you see a man obviously trying to guide the short putt or hitting quickly with a short, stabbing stroke, even though he holes a few, if you look for trouble you will not be disappointed. A short putt, even as a long one, must be struck with a smooth, unhurried, and confident stroke. The best way to accomplish this is to decide upon a line to the hole and determine to hit the ball on that line and let it go hang if it wants to. I have never had any better advice in golf from tee to green than was contained in a telegram sent me by Stewart Maiden in 1919. It read: "Hit 'em hard. They'll land somewhere." You must not apply this advice literally to putting, but its application is obvious. Hit the putt as well as you can and do not allow worry over the outcome to spoil the stroke.

In this connection it is worthy of observation that nearly everyone finds it easier to stroke properly a putt of twelve to fifteen feet. There is a very good reason why this should be true. The player fears he will miss a shorter putt and he fears he may fail to lay a longer one dead, but when he is putting from the middle distance he merely hopes he may hole out without feeling that he must guide the ball into the hole and he knows that he will not likely take three putts.

We would all profit greatly if we could cultivate this attitude toward putts of all lengths, and it ought to be easy to do, too, for we all know, or should know by this time, that worry does very little good. If we must be wrong we may as well make our mistake gracefully by choosing the wrong line as by allowing a nervous, overcareful stroke to pull the ball off direction.

CHIP VS. PUTT

Someone wonders and asks why, since he chips well, does he not enjoy an equal proficiency once he is actually on the putting surface. Are not putts and chip shots played in the same way, the latter being merely a bit longer and played with a lofted club?

For years I worked on exactly this theory. I provided myself with a run-up club, an old-fashioned cleek with a short shaft, which was to all intents and purposes a lofted putter. I began to use this club for all chipping and run-up shots, and always attempted to swing the club exactly as I was in the habit of swinging a putter.

But I found in time a number of reasons why a chip shot cannot be regarded and played as an extended putt. I still carry the little cleek and find good use for it on the keen approaches of seaside golf in Britain, but I no longer attempt to swing it like a putter.

In the first place, almost all of the important part of putting takes place within a radius of forty feet from the hole, and this usually over a keen green, where delicacy and meticulous accuracy is needed.

In the first place, almost all of the important part of putting takes place within a radius of forty feet from the hole, and this usually over a keen green, where delicacy and meticulous accuracy is needed. For this reason a light, sensitive grip must be cultivated, and in the position of address considerations of accuracy must be allowed to prevail over the accommodation of extended motion. In other words the putting style and grip are developed to suit best the shorter ranges rather than to facilitate a stroke from the outermost edge of the green. The player naturally handles his putter more easily within forty feet than outside that limit.

Diegel's Distinctive Style.

Almost every player makes a decided difference between his putting method and his manner of playing a shot from fifty yards off the green. Consider Leo Diegel, for instance. Is it possible to picture Diegel employing his crablike putting style from any considerable distance? Such a thing would be absurd. Yet Diegel is a fine putter. I think the better view is that putting is a game in itself, and chipping, instead of being an extension of putting, is an abbreviation of iron play.

> I play most of my short chips when only
> a few feet off the edge of the putting
> surface with a mashie-iron, but I chip
> with any iron club from the mashie-iron
> down to a niblick, depending upon
> what relation I desire to maintain
> between the pitch and the run.

To illustrate by my own experience, I employ the same grip from tee to green. I drive, play the irons, pitch, and chip holding the club in the same way. But I alter my grip considerably once I have the ball on the green. I play most of my short chips when only a few feet off the edge of the putting surface with a mashie-iron, but I chip with any iron club from the mashie-iron down to a niblick, depending upon what relation I desire to maintain between the pitch and the run.

The element of backspin is sometimes important in chipping. It is occasionally desired to play the shot with a slight dragging spin in order to limit the roll of the ball. This, of course, cannot be accomplished by the gentle, sweeping stroke of the putter, but must be effected by a longer, more crisply delivered blow. The club must be held in a more capable grip and the posture be such that unlimited motion can be accommodated easily.

Keep Putting Separate.

It is further possible to chip very well using always a slight cut accomplished by drawing the face of the club across the ball, nipping the sphere neatly at the point where it rests on the ground. I do not need to say how far removed that is from good putting practice.

> He may consider if he likes that in chipping he is merely reducing the iron stroke to miniature, but let him not attempt to extend his putting to embrace anything else.

It is difficult to say when a chip outgrows its classification and becomes a run-up or a pitch. There is no sharp dividing line where one leaves off and the other begins. But there is a very definite separation of putting from anything else in the game, and the player will do well to observe the distinction. He may consider if he likes that in chipping he is merely reducing the iron stroke to miniature, but let him not attempt to extend his putting to embrace anything else.

A Correct Sequence
to Every Shot

It is often urged that a person playing golf who worries about how to take the club back, how to start it down and what to do at this stage and at that, ultimately loses sight of the only important thing he has to do—to hit the ball. We, who write on the game and attempt to teach it, are told often enough that we should give more attention to the contact stage and less to the details of the preparatory motions.

It is true, of course, that it is not impossible to hit an occasional good shot even though all the teachings and practice of the experts in fundamentals are disregarded. But one who takes the long-range viewpoint cannot fail to appreciate that the basis of consistent and reliable performance must be good form. There are certain actions which must take place during the act of hitting if the ball is to be struck with accuracy and power. A haphazard, uninformed player, once in a while may find himself in position to complete these actions, but he cannot hope to compete successfully with the man whose sound swing carries him time after time into this position.

A Correct Sequence.

The downward or hitting stroke is intended to culminate in a well-timed, powerful contact between clubhead and ball.

16

There is no way to argue that the successful accomplishment of this purpose is not the most important part of the stroke.

> It is beyond all reasonable expectations
> that a person may hole a chip shot,
> so little will be gained by playing
> always for the hole.

But the backswing has for its purpose the establishment of a perfectly balanced, powerful position at the top of the swing from which the correct actions of the downstroke can flow rhythmically without the need for interference or correction.

In the end, on the basis of consistent reproduction of the successful action, the preparatory movements become just as important as the actual hitting—the entire swing, a sequence of correct positions, following naturally and comfortably one after the other.

I think it is easier to understand the requirements of a good backswing if one looks first at the things which it is designed to accomplish. And in this case it is fortunate that the position is not posed but pictures the extension incident to an actual driving swing. The important points are the left arm, the left shoulder, the turns of the body, and the cock of the wrists. The fact that the hands are higher than the head, and the shaft of the club is pointing to the right of the objective is also worth noting.

Straight Left Arm Governs Arc.

The straightness of the left arm accomplishes, or at least makes possible, a number of desirable things. First and most important, its full extension, maintained throughout from the start of the backswing until impact, causes the arc of the swing

17

to be very wide, and this increases its potential power. Likewise, since the distance from the left shoulder to the left hand is constant so long as the left elbow remains unbent, the straight left, in the only possible way, locates the arm of the swing where it can be retraced times without number. It is plain from the photograph, too, that the left arm owes its opportunity to remain straight to the fact that the right arm is relaxed and is a willing follower.

> I think crouching is the worst mistake
> the average person makes when
> playing a chip shot.

This suggests what I deem to be the proper procedure, namely, that the club should be swung back mainly by pushing it with the left arm. This tends to avoid the common mistake of picking the club up abruptly with the right hand, and likewise materially encourages a free turn of the hips and shoulders.

It will be seen also that the shoulders have not turned in the same plane. The left shoulder is now several inches lower than the right, whereas it was itself higher when addressing the ball. The turn has been very full, but dipping the left shoulder has permitted the location of the head and the axis of the shoulders to remain unchanged.

PICTURE THE SHOT FIRST

It is always important in playing golf that there should be in the mind of the player a definite picture of what he intends to do with the clubhead. It is safe to say that a vast majority of the struggling multitude are able to conjure up no very accurate conception of the swing. As they stand before the ball their minds are utterly confused with all the do's and don'ts they can think of jumbled together. Even if a picture which they might have should contain a few inaccuracies, still they would be better off than with no plan at all.

One thing which has led to trouble has been the effort made by so many to "throw the clubhead at the ball," especially when there has been trouble with slicing, a fault to which most inexpert players are addicted. It is never difficult to attribute a badly cut shot to late hitting—that is, to a failure to bring the face of the club around quickly enough—and the most obvious means of correction is by holding the hands back and whipping the clubhead through.

The chief trouble with this procedure is that it almost always exaggerates the mistake sought to be avoided or results in smothering, which is worse. This is one place where the inside-out theory should be given a chance, not as a thing to be actually accomplished but as an end toward which to strive in order to correct the slice.

The picture which I like to have in mind is one of hitting directly along the line of flight, with the face of the club

d to the hole, and in order to accomplish this
ound it very helpful to "see" my hands slightly
e clubhead at impact. The club face having
ing the backswing must, of course, be closed
g down, but this operation can be and should be
handled by the left hand without any necessity for holding
the hands back. It is obviously impossible to hit from the inside out or even along the line of flight, if the clubhead is allowed to get in front of the hands before the ball is struck.

Leo Diegel, when he is having one of his good days, is
probably the most accurate iron-player in the world. I have
seen him on occasions when each iron shot looked as
though it would knock the flag out of the hole and it is characteristic of Diegel on such an occasion that his hands are
perceptibly ahead of the club. The impression which one
gains from watching him is that the club is being pulled
through with the left side.

There are several things recognized as part and parcel of
good form which the hands-in-front picture automatically
takes care of. This one idea, besides suggesting a blow in the
right direction, also assures that the punch will be slightly
downward and that the weight of the body will flow forward
into the stroke. The attempt to whip the clubhead through
ahead of the hands usually sets the player back upon his
right foot, a mistake which should never be allowed.

As in every other thing pertaining to the golf stroke, exaggeration in this respect must be avoided. There are players
who actually do permit the clubhead to lag too far behind,
but it will pay a person troubled with slicing to examine his
swing and find out if he is not holding his hands and his
body back too much. Among the expert players it is not uncommon at all to find the hands as much as three or four
inches beyond the ball at impact and I do not recall a single
case which shows the clubhead ahead of the hands at this
point.

ON THE DIFFERENT METHODS
FOR AN IRON SHOT

The question whether or not there is any great difference between the best method for an iron shot and that for a drive often recurs. It is said, "Would it not be simple to swing all clubs alike? Is there any real reason for a difference?"

> Playing an iron, an exact control of distance is most desirable, while in driving and, at least half the time, in playing a wood club from the fairway it is length, and as much as possible of it, which is sought.

The principal reason why there must be a difference is that in the two cases it is not the ideal that the ball should behave in the same way. Playing an iron, an exact control of distance is most desirable, while in driving and, at least half the time, in playing a wood club from the fairway it is length, and as much as possible of it, which is sought. In the first instance, backspin is an aid both in holding the flight of the ball true and in limiting its run after it strikes the ground; but off the tee, and through the green where the ultimate length is desired, the ball must be made to roll as far as possible. A golf hole requires a tee shot to be well placed, but the occasion rarely arises when the longer shot, properly directed, is not better than the shorter one.

> The backspin with which an iron is
> played is accomplished by striking a
> downward blow with a lofted club.

The backspin with which an iron is played is accomplished by striking a downward blow with a lofted club. The way in which the club takes the ball first and then passes into the turf in front of the spot where the ball rested is familiar to everyone. In order to drive a ball without backspin, this downward punch is omitted and the club swings in a sweeping arc which is flatter at the bottom, and should strike the ball squarely in the back while the clubhead is moving in a horizontal plane. In this way the spinning effect is limited to the loft on the face of the club.

The tee shot which is knocked down will invariably climb when bucking any sort of contrary breeze. The downward blow produces backspin and this spin forces the ball up. When its force is spent it descends almost vertically and usually drops dead. And the player, having noted a sweet feel and an attractive-looking shot is surprised to find himself yards behind another drive which did not look to be nearly as good as his. I think it is a misunderstanding of the principle which makes the man who has only a little knowledge so helpless in a heavy wind. Trying to keep his shots down makes him hit them with backspin. They start out low enough, but rise quickly and soon are floating at the mercy of the wind.

Along this same line it is hard to make a beginner understand that the best way to get a brassie shot up from a close or cuppy lie is to "go down after it." Given a lie of this kind, slightly downhill, the average golfer wants to pick the ball cleanly and lift it up. His reward is usually a full or half-top.

The experienced player makes no such mistake. He knows that he cannot obtain his greatest length in this way, but he must get the ball up to get any length at all. So, instead of trying to take the ball cleanly he smashes it down and relies upon the spin to cause it to rise.

> Along this same line it is hard to make a beginner understand that the best way to get a brassie shot up from a close or cuppy lie is to "go down after it.

Almost all beginners are slicers and nearly all slicers strike downward. Very few players who hook habitually hit down. They are usually slightly more advanced and need only to use their left sides a bit more to play very creditable games.

ON THE BENEFITS OF
BASIC GOLF INSTRUCTION

A s I come in contact with more and more so-called average golfers there is one remark I once heard which keeps coming back to me. An old-timer was asked why a certain youngster, who had shown promise for some while, was not improving more rapidly, "What's the matter, isn't he ambitious?"

> I do not urge that every man, woman, or child who begins to play golf should immediately plunge into a serious study of the subject with the aim of becoming a great player.

"Certainly he's ambitious," was the reply. "He would like best in the world to be champion of the United States. But he isn't willing to do the work it takes to make him that." And so a great many people like to play golf; they would like to play reasonably well, without any thought of championships, of course, but they are not willing to do the work.

Of course it is easy to understand why a man who plays only an occasional round and is too busy with other affairs to give much time to the game is unwilling to spend hour after hour practicing or taking lessons. When he goes out he plays with friends of about the same ability as himself and has a grand time. But even he finds a keen thrill in every well-hit shot, and in refusing to give himself any chance for improvement he is actually denying himself the greater joy which the game could give him.

I do not urge that every man, woman, or child who begins to play golf should immediately plunge into a serious study of the subject with the aim of becoming a great player. Fortunately the game is too fine for that. Such a course is open to any who have the time and inclination to follow it, and it is a course which may be run through ever-changing scenery during the longest lifetime. But the person who plays a casual round now and then and merely aspires to play moderately well is not likely to delight in the game as a subject for much study and experiment.

> There is no reason in the world why a competent instructor could not in a few short lessons instruct a pupil in a number of fundamentals which would help him to play better and give him more pleasure without making the thing a drudgery for him.

In a few rare cases it might happen that a person would make fair progress at the game without assistance other than that he might gain from watching others. But if we exclude the child with a faculty for imitation who trails around behind a first-class professional I think we would find these instances very rare.

But where a player of this latter class makes his mistake is in thinking that in order to absorb any amount of instruction he must involve himself in a lot of complicated theories. One may find many of them who because they fear they may be asked to slave at the game steadfastly refuse to be advised in any particular. In some cases even, I am afraid, this refusal may be caused by the apprehension that they may be thought to take the game more seriously than they should or than the results which they would be able to get would justify.

When one stops to take stock it is difficult not to be surprised at the number of intelligent people who like to play golf and have played at it for quite a long while without ever taking the trouble to find out how to hold the club. There is no reason in the world why a competent instructor could not in a few short lessons instruct a pupil in a number of fundamentals which would help him to play better and give him more pleasure without making the thing a drudgery for him. If he has no desire to go beyond that, let him go on and play with his friends. At least he will have a chance to go somewhere and not be condemned to hack the ball about the course for the rest of his existence, or until he gives up golf.

VARIANCES IN CLUB-FITTING

Every so often a letter comes to me inquiring about as follows: "I am so many feet tall, weigh so much, am so many years old and am (or am not) very strong. What length clubs would you recommend?" I should get up a form letter to send in reply, for there is really no intelligent advice which can be given to the individual. Those who find the standard lengths unsatisfactory know better than anyone else in which direction they would like to make a departure, whether to increase or decrease the length, and apparently height and build have very little to do with the question.

A tall man does not necessarily require longer clubs than the short man. This problem is controlled by a number of factors beyond this, by the position he prefers; that is, by the degree of bend which he finds most comfortable, by the distance from the ball which he likes to maintain, and by the breadth of arc which gives him the best balance between distance and control. In short, the determining factor is comfort. There is no rule that so many inches of height require so many inches of club.

Since the advent of the steel-shaft golf club, lengths have been more or less standarized. It never was a good idea to alter the length of any kind of club which left the manufacturer's or clubmaker's hands perfectly balanced. Such a procedure has become even less a good idea now, because the steel cannot be scraped or pared down to restore the feel destroyed by decreasing the length. But the necessity that the player balance length and control in the selection of a club has enabled the manufacturers of steel-shafted clubs to arrive at standard lengths which are suitable to almost all individuals. They could never have done this if it had been true that the length of the club had to vary in direct proportion to the length of the player.

Back in the times when everyone was using hickory I remember being surprised on discovering that Long Jim Barnes' driver was a shade shorter than my own, and some time later, on learning that Wee Bobby Cruickshank's was some little longer. Evidently in these cases the lengths of the clubs used by two men of almost a foot difference in stature had been brought to almost the same point (I understand Cruickshank is now using standard length woods) by the balance of control and length. Barnes, with his great height, was able to get all the arc he could control with the shorter club, and Cruickshank needed a comparatively longer club to get the distance.

Many men of short stature have experimented with abnormally long clubs. Cruickshank was one of these, but if I am informed correctly he has now given it up. There is one fine player in England who carries a fifty-inch driver, but he rarely uses it, because it is not easily controllable. I used to use long shafts in my irons, but cut them off in 1926 at Tommy Armour's suggestion, and found my iron play much improved.

I have rarely run across a club in any man's bag to which I could not accommodate myself, the lengths have been so little different from my own. But I regard this as a phenomenon which by no means alters the fact that shaft lengths are to be determined wholly on the basis of individual preference. My chief warning is to avoid the idea that height and reach, or either, are the controlling factors. Comfort is the main thing, and a tall man need not be surprised if he likes a short club, or a short man a long one.

ON THE CURE FOR
"LOOKING UP" IN THE STROKE

Golf is recognized as one of the most difficult games to play or teach. One reason for this is that each person necessarily plays by feel, and a feeling is almost impossible to describe. Another reason is found in the fact that certain things which are necessary to be done cannot be attacked directly, but must be made right while directing the attention to something else.

> This is carried a step further by some of those who have noticed that the first-class player, in playing a normal stroke, keeps his head down for a perceptible interval after he strikes the ball.

It has been my experience that the admonition to hold the head still and "keep your eye on the ball" in most cases comes under this latter heading. For almost anyone, attempting to fix his eye upon the ball or to hold his head immovable, soon finds himself so full of tension that he is helpless.

I have occasionally run across a person who said that he was helped by selecting a particular point on the surface of the ball at which to look. But the pros and better amateurs will always tell you that they do not consciously fix their gaze upon any particular point nor, indeed, upon the ball at all. They are merely aware of the location of the ball. They are no doubt seeing it during the entire stroke, but they do not stare at it.

This is carried a step further by some of those who have noticed that the first-class player, in playing a normal stroke, keeps his head down for a perceptible interval after he strikes the ball. Some interpret this as an indication that there is an effort to keep the gaze upon the spot from which the ball has departed, in an effort to avoid looking up too quickly. Yet this is hardly ever the case. I doubt if one of these men would ever be aware that he had not the ball in sight from the moment his backswing began until the flight of the ball had ended or had carried beyond an obstruction where it was no longer visible.

The danger of "looking up" apparently becomes greater as the length of the shot becomes less. Rarely do we see an indication of "looking up" when the player is driving or playing an iron shot. Sometimes the head comes up and the shot is spoiled, but I think this is caused more by a resistance elsewhere in the stroke forcing the head away than by failing to look at the ball. In other words, the head lifting itself results from a mechanical fault, and does not itself start the trouble.

> On the putting green, however, the player's chief concern just before he begins his stroke is to align the face of his club exactly; and the head of the putter remains always before his eye.

In chipping and putting there may be this difference. Within the hitting areas is where the club is most likely to distract the eye when playing a full shot; the clubhead is moving so fast that little interference can result. On the putting green, however, the player's chief concern just before he begins his stroke is to align the face of his club exactly; and the head of the putter remains always before his eye. There is danger then of distracting, not so much his eye or gaze, but his attention from the ball.

Only recently I experienced a spell of bad putting which, I finally determined, was due solely to a habit of following the putter blade with my eye as it moved away from the ball. Of course, the only cure was to refuse to allow my gaze to be drawn away, but even then it was more a matter of refusing to worry about the putter than of looking at the ball. It would have been the same if the hole or the line had been drawing my attention. There is nothing more necessary for good putting than to make two entirely separate operations of deciding upon the line and striking the ball. It is best always to have the first job out of the way so that the entire attention can be given to the second.

IMPORTANCE OF A
SMOOTH SHORT GAME

One of the qualities most to be desired in a golf stroke is smoothness, and smoothness becomes impossible unless the backswing is amply long to allow time for gradual acceleration of the club in coming down. A backswing that is too short brings about the necessity of making a sudden effort in the act of hitting. Bridging the gap between zero velocity and maximum in the shorter space implies hurry and effort, which can very easily destroy the rhythm of the stroke. Such a procedure is directly opposed to the motion of swinging the clubhead.

Nowhere is the disastrous effect of a short backswing more easily noted than in the play on and around the greens. Here, particularly, where smooth stroking is absolutely essential, the short, choppy stroke soon leaves its perpetrator entirely helpless. Some men have become good holers-out, employing a short backswing and a distinct hit in the stroke—that is, they have had a fair amount of success in getting the ball into the hole from the shorter distances on reasonably flat greens. But those who putt in this way invariably have difficulty with the longer putts and on keen, undulating greens, where a delicate touch is of first importance. The man who takes a short, sharp rap at the ball will never be able to compete in these respects with the putter who swings the club.

Almost always I am able to trace my putting troubles to an abbreviated or too rapid backswing. Whenever I am swinging the club back smoothly and in a broad sweep without hurry I am confident of putting well. When I am not doing so I know I will putt badly. The shorter backswing makes me hit sharply and jerkily without a chance to control the force of the blow. The stroke which I like, especially on greens that are keen and true, is one which appears to float the club into the ball and gently waves it over the smooth surface. Such a stroke is pleasing to the eye and the sense of feel and it is very reliable.

The same thing applies with equal force to chipping and other short approach work. Billy Burke, one of the finest short-game players in the world, has said that he makes a point of swinging back even a little farther than necessary when playing the first few chips of any round. He recognizes the importances of an ample backswing and feels that it is easier to make sure of it at the start than to work into it from the other direction.

It is never very difficult for the player himself to feel the jerk in his swing when he has one. Whenever he becomes conscious of a nervous, jittery stroke on or around the greens, let him look first to his backswing. The easiest way back to smoothness and confidence is to swing the club leisurely and amply.

DAY-TO-DAY ADJUSTMENTS

Playing on the National Golf Links not very long ago, I happened to be driving very well. Alec Girard, the club professional, walking around with us, asked if there was any one thing I thought about that enabled me to keep on hitting the ball where I wanted it. I replied that when I was hitting the ball well, there were always one or two things which I made certain of doing, and the doing of them would assure success for a while. But they were not always the same things. One conception was good for only a limited time, and when the charm wore off, I would have to begin looking for something else. Alec said emphatically that his experience had been the same.

This is one of the things which our theorists and analysts overlook when they are not themselves reasonably capable players. It is of great value to have a clear understanding of the successive movements which make up a correct golf swing. This much is needed in order to enable one to recognize and correct faults as they appear. But no human is able to think through and at the same time execute the entire sequence of correct movements. The player himself must seek for a conception or fix upon one or two movements on which to concentrate, which will enable him to hit the ball. And then when this wears out, because, perhaps, he begins to exaggerate or overemphasize it to the detriment of something else, the search must begin anew for another idea which will work. In this process there inevitably are alterations in the swing, not in fundamentals, of course, nor of radical proportions, but more than can be accounted for in any series of diagrams.

If the expert player, possessing a swing that is sound in fundamentals, has to be continually jockeying about to find the means of making it produce fine golf shots, what of the average golfer who has never developed such a swing? Still groping for some sort of method which will give him some measure of reliability, it is only natural that he should try almost anything. If he ever wants to improve he must strive in every way possible to build up a sound style.

There is a whole lot in knowing what to monkey with and what to leave alone. In making day-to-day adjustments I never consider even for a moment making any alteration, however slight, in my grip. It is of the utmost importance that the hands should be placed on the club so that they can perform certain necessary functions and the correct grip should be the first thing learned. But after this has been done the accustomed feel of the club should never be altered. It is only through the grip that the player is able to sense the location of the clubhead and the alignment of the face. If he is constantly changing here, he cannot possibly retain this feel. The temptation is great sometimes to correct a temporary hooking or slicing tendency by shifting the right hand more over or under the club. This should never be done. If the grip is wrong, change it by all means, but let the change be a permanent one.

The stance can vary considerably, shifting the feet to favor a hook or a slice; the ball can be shifted about within ample limits with respect to the feet. These little changes are by no means fundamental. Even what might didactically be prescribed as the correct swing allows some latitude in these matters.

The important thing which the nongolfing theorist or analyst can seldom appreciate is the importance of the player's conception of how to put the correct swing to work. Very often what a man feels that he is doing is more important than what he does. The feel, the experience, is so much easier to remember and repeat. When you arrive at a feeling of doing something in any part of the stroke and that something continues to produce good results, you will have a player's conception to hang onto. It is something upon which to concentrate and which everyone must have in order to play consistent golf. Even the soundest swing must have some simple control to keep it in order.

Don't Tinker with a Sound Grip

In considering golfing "tips" and their worth, or rather lack of worth, one cannot help thinking of the favorite quick cure for a hook or slice involving the shifting of the position of the right hand upon the club. The right hand more under the shaft to correct a slice and more over to correct a hook. It is familiar music, of course, but if there ever was a pure "tip" having no relation to the promulgation of sound golfing information this is it.

A correct grip is a fundamental necessity in the correct swing. It might even be said to be the first necessity, for a person must take hold of the club before he can swing it and he must hold it correctly before it becomes physically possible for him to swing it correctly. But there was never a more pernicious thought in golf than that the grip is something to go tinkering with in order to counteract some mistake made in swinging, for which it was not responsible. Few average golfers or duffers grip the club correctly. Most of them should alter the position of one hand or the other, or of both, but the change should be permanent and not merely as a temporary corrective.

I began playing golf at the age of six, with the interlocking grip. I played in this way for about two years and then changed over to the overlapping. So far as I know my grip now is precisely as it was when I was eight years old or nine, whenever it was I made this change. Since that time, I have experimented with changes, in order to correct temporary faults, just enough to know that they do more harm than good.

> The difference is not far removed from
> that which I find between myself, as a
> dub billiard player, and a true expert.

In the correct grip the two hands should be able to function as nearly as possible as one, and their positions on the club should encourage easy handling of the club throughout a correct swing. If a player is not in the habit of employing a grip which fills this bill, he should immediately alter it until it does. But after altering this grip until it is correct and comfortable let him resolve never to change it. If something goes wrong let him look elsewhere for the trouble. For the hands form the connection with the club. Through the hands the player is able to sense the location and alignment of the club. They are the keys to his control. The slightest change leaves him groping.

The worst mistake possible to make in gripping the club is to separate the actions of the two hands. It is not necessary to distinguish between the overlapping, interlocking and old-fashioned grips. Either one is good enough if the hands are placed so they can work together.

Some little latitude is allowable, but it will be seen to be very small. The left hand must be in a position of power; it must be placed so that it can swing the club through without jamming the left elbow against the side. It must, therefore, be well up on top of the shaft. The beginner who holds his club so that he can see the tips of the fingers of his left hand is hopeless until he changes.

Similarly the right hand must not be placed too far under the shaft, for starting from this position, it is likely to turn over in the act of hitting. If the left hand has been placed correctly, it is not likely that the right will be placed too much on top, for this would require a contortion which no one is likely to endure in order to cause himself trouble.

The correct grip can be demonstrated more easily than it can be described. I should recommend to any player who is not absolutely sure that he is right, that he check his grip immediately with a competent instructor. Until he is right here he is not ready for anything else.

ON THE POSITION OF THE FEET AT ADDRESS

I remember one night at the Marine Hotel in Gullane, Scotland, back in 1926, when the British Amateur was being played at Muirfield, George Duncan was expounding to a few of us his latest theory of the golf swing. George expressed the belief that the most important part of the business was accomplished by the knees and feet. He described and illustrated for us how he was "playing golf with his feet"; the "take-off" from the left foot originating the motion of the backswing.

> It is too easy to set down one foot in
> such a position that it will embarrass
> the stroke without being aware of the
> mistake until the swing has gotten
> under way, which is, of course, too late.

Without either subscribing to or denying the correctness of Duncan's ideas—indeed, I think they might be helpful to some as well as ruinous for others—it is safe to say that a great many players allow their feet to spoil too many shots. It is too easy to set down one foot in such a position that it will embarrass the stroke without being aware of the mistake until the swing has gotten under way, which is, of course, too late. A little more care in intelligently cultivating the habit of proper placing will be well rewarded.

And in this I am not speaking entirely of the location of the feet with respect to each other. Almost everyone has found out that a more open stance—with right foot advanced—encourages a slice or fade, and that a closed stance—with left foot advanced—is responsible for an opposite tendency. But the thing goes farther than that, to the placing of each foot upon the ground in the proper relation to the leg, the body, and the swing.

Almost everyone has found out that a more open stance—with right foot advanced—encourages a slice or fade, and that a closed stance—with left foot advanced—is responsible for an opposite tendency.

I may as well say right here that I am one of those who favor a very generous hip-turn. In my own swing the hips turn during the backswing for a full shot through almost 90 degrees until my back is presented toward the hole. And then they turn through very fast in hitting. Now there is only one way in which I can place my feet which will not cause one of them to hamper the hip action going one way or the other. That is, each one must occupy approximately the position— each with the toe turned slightly outward so that the center line of each foot makes an angle of about 20 degrees (no more with a line drawn perpendicular to the line of flight). I find that this position can be altered a little bit for the right foot—it may even point directly forward, exactly across the line of flight—but that the placing of the left foot must be fairly definite. To see why this is, one need only try a few swings with the left foot pointed toward the hole or in a pigeon-toed position. The first will be found to make impossible a free turn of the hips backward, while the second will interfere seriously with the turn through the ball.

> There is no need to set down any of
> these observations except to say that I
> have noted that everyone who makes
> a considerable use of his hips,
> in a turning action, places his left
> foot about as I do.

It has been interesting to me, since hearing Duncan, to observe the way various players handle their feet and to note the relation of such handling to the rest of the swing. There is no need to set down any of these observations except to say that I have noted that everyone who makes a considerable use of his hips, in a turning action, places his left foot about as I do. Leo Diegel is the only exception I can recall offhand. Leo's left foot points almost squarely to the front as a rule, but I suspect that he finds the position a bit uncomfortable—at least, subconsciously—because as he hits the ball the foot almost invariably swings around more toward the hole.

WHAT'S RIGHT ABOUT RHYTHM

Smoothness is the keynote of the successful golf swing. The man with a faulty swing ties himself up to an extent that makes a smooth stroke impossible. The expert swings smoothly because his successive positions are easy and comfortable, and are such that the movement from one to the other is not hampered by unwilling muscles. The average golfer does not swing smoothly because at some stage he creates a condition which makes it easier for him to move in the wrong direction than in the right one.

Here is an example of how one faulty position or movement can upset a swing, which, with this one fault corrected, is able to function reasonably well. The swing, being my own, is one with which I can claim to be fairly familiar. And the trouble I have had recently marks the first time in at least ten years when I have developed a fault which I could not detect and work out for myself within a reasonable time.

Strikes a New Fault.

For several months now the old feeling of comfort and smoothness has entirely escaped me, especially with the woods—the irons have not been so bad. I have noted that my swing was abnormally fast, and particularly that my legs were not working just right. I have tried everything that has worked in the past—slowing down, exaggerating the forward shift of my hips coming down, watching the wrist cock to make certain of getting the left side into the stroke, but still I could not bring back the accustomed rhythm. I did suspect that the trouble was in my feet, for I could not be even nearly comfortable in the stance and position, which on examination I knew to be my usual ones.

So, despairing of ever working the thing out myself, I took George Sargent out to knock around a few holes and talk the thing over. At first of course he could only see that my swing did not look like it used to look, that the rhythm was gone, and that it lacked power. Searching back from effect to cause, after we had played five holes, he happened to be standing directly behind my back as I hit a brassie shot. Immediately he caught it. In addressing the ball, my right heel was entirely off the ground.

Smooth Back Difficult.

Now, let's see what the effect of this would be. My right knee was bent abnormally and what weight rested on the right foot was supported on the toe. Obviously, this made a normal stance, with both feet about on line, very uncomfortable. With only the toe of this foot supporting the weight, I had to draw the right foot well back to maintain any sort of balance. But the worst part of it was that the precarious balance made an even smooth start back impossible. There was an irresistible impulse to get back to earth quickly, and my backswing always started with a jerk. Straightening the right leg a bit—it should never be perfectly straight or rigid at the beginning—and lowering the right heel to the ground has made my balance certain again, and I am able to start back without hurry.

The two points where smoothness is in most danger are at

the start of the backswing and at the start of the downstroke. To start back smoothly avoids haste later on, and to start down in leisurely fashion maintains the perfect balance and provides for well-timed, accurate striking.

AN EASY SOLUTION
TO EXTRA YARDS

We have all been told often enough that relaxed muscles and a rhythmic swing are two essentials for the execution of a successful golf shot. More particularly these are the essentials of any stroke which is intended to drive the ball any considerable distance. Yet how many times do we see this knowledge disregarded by players who ought to know better, when the exigencies of a particular situation suggest the desirability of a few extra yards.

There are two main tendencies which the average player exhibits when he wants to hit hard. First, he is impelled to widen his stance, and second, to place himself further from the ball where he has the feeling that he can really "swing on it." In most cases, too, he will plant his feet firmly in the turf in order to complete what he considers "setting himself" for the stroke. And then he slugs at the ball and wonders why he doesn't achieve the enormous shot he had intended.

If one will take the trouble to observe, he will notice certain things which are characteristic of all true swingers of a golf club. First, that the posture of the body at address is fairly erect and that the location of the ball is near enough so that there is no need to stretch out for it; second, that the feet are not separated so widely that the movement of the hips is restricted and that they are not rooted into the ground. The whole picture will be one of apparent ease and comfort, entirely free from strain of any kind. And this is the beginning of a swing which will get distance and control.

Spreading the feet to an abnormal span ties up the mid-section of the body, so that the possibility of a free turn of the hips—a source of great power—is entirely removed. The golfer must maintain a perfect balance but what he wants is a balance in motion, and not a firm planting which will resist strong and outside forces. Aside from wind pressure, he has only to balance his own movements and the forces he himself sets up, and the occasional necessity of bracing against a strong wind is small excuse for tying up one's swing eternally.

So, also, for the practice of standing a great distance away from the ball. What the spreading of the feet does for the hip region, so do the extension of the arms and bending of the body for the muscles of the arms, shoulders, and upper back. The long drivers stand noticeably erect, and their arms are permitted to hang easily from the shoulders. They place themselves at the outset where they are able to utilize every ounce of power which it is possible to derive from an ample turn of the body.

I grant willingly that there are times when one must have just a little more length than he would feel like trying for normally. It is not a good idea to strive for the ultimate length off every tee, but it is a fine thing to be able to produce a few extra yards when they are needed. But this additional can never be had by stretching and slugging. On the contrary, it is obtained more easily by increasing the turn and use of the hips and shoulders.

THE POSTURE AT ADDRESS

In my last article I said something about how an easy comfortable posture at address could aid in dispelling the tension so often present when the golfer prepares to make a stroke. I suggested that three errors at this point were common, namely, a too wide stance (feet too widely separated), too much bend in the body over the ball, and a more or less rigid extension of the arms beyond their natural hanging positions. I think that all three are important enough to watch carefully.

I suppose that if one feature of my own style has attracted any notice it is that my feet are very close together during the execution of every shot from the full drive on down.

I suppose that if one feature of my own style has attracted any notice it is that my feet are very close together during the execution of every shot from the full drive on down. I am quite certain that my heels in playing any shot are never separated by more than twelve inches without some loss of effectiveness except, of course, where the character of the ground makes an unusual stance necessary, and as I near the hole this distance grows less. This was at first, of course, quite a natural or an accidental procedure, a characteristic developed without thought on my part, although it likely was one of the many features attributed to my imitation of Stewart Maiden. But I have found since that it is as fundamental a part of my game as anything could be.

Allows Ample Body Turn.

So long as my feet remain close together I have free use of my hips and shoulders, and an ample body turn is a simple affair, easy to accomplish fully and without loss of balance. But sometimes when there is a temptation to stretch out a bit in an effort to add a few yards on the end of a drive, the right foot begins to creep back a little bit further away from the left (there is somehow the feeling that this is necessary when one wants to hit exceptionally hard) and the stance widens out by several inches. This never fails to tie me up. The wider stance locks my hips, they cannot turn so easily, and this leads to a hurried backswing and an unsatisfactory shot.

It does not require much argument to show that the other two faults I have mentioned are equally troublesome in producing tension. The player who bends well over the ball likewise places himself in such a position that a free body turn is impossible. The only way he could accomplish it would be by first rising to a more erect position. As a matter of fact, I have seen a great many do just this, even after starting the swing, producing a sort of rolling motion, up and down, and a turn which is not a hip turn at all, but one of the entire physical mechanism from the ground up.

Don't Reach for Ball.

The man who reaches out for the ball gets into trouble because he cannot extend his arms and remain relaxed. The extreme of this is often seen in the fellow who extends his arms and elevates his hands until arms, hands, and club complete a straight line from his shoulders to the ball. The teaching that the left arm and the club should lie in the same vertical plane is all right, but no one in his wildest moments ever conceived that they should lie in a plane in any other direction.

I always like to see a person stand up to a golf ball as though he were perfectly at home in its presence, in a posture which appears easy and comfortable from top to bottom. To accomplish this it is only necessary to stand erect, with feet just far enough apart to accommodate a little footwork when the body is turned from side to side. Then bend over slightly, just enough to assure that when the arms are hung naturally downward the hands will have free passage across the front of the body.

From this posture, movement in any direction is easy. There is nothing straining about it. The comfort of the position encourages relaxation. The player can take a club in his hand and swing it as freely and as hard as ever he likes without upsetting his balance.

ON KEEPING THE CHIN
BACK AT ADDRESS

Someone asked me the other day if I was conscious of looking at the ball with my left eye rather than with my right. I replied that I was not, and that if I looked at the ball with either eye it was a habit of such long standing that I no longer thought about it. "But," the man insisted, "I have noticed that you and Walter Hagen and a good many of the other fellows hold your heads in such a position that you appear to be looking at the ball with the left eye. Surely there must be some reason for or advantage to be derived from the practice. I should like to know what it is."

> I have never attached much importance to the "master eye" theory. I don't think it makes any difference which of a man's eyes is the stronger or whether he gazes at any particular point on the cover of the ball. All that he needs is to be able to measure the distance and to locate accurately the ball's position.

I confess that the position of my head when preparing to hit a golf ball is entirely distinctive. I began to do it long before I ever gave a thought to style or the mechanics of the stroke. I believe the same thing to be true in Hagen's case. But several years ago I did have demonstrated to me the importance of the head position in its effect upon the rest of the stroke. I have never attached much importance to the "master eye" theory. I don't think it makes any difference which of a man's eyes is the stronger or whether he gazes at any particular point on the cover of the ball. All that he needs is to be able to measure the distance and to locate accurately the ball's position. I am told that he can do this better with two eyes than with one.

> Alex Morrison, more than anyone else, I think, has harped upon the "chin-back" idea. I am convinced that it is sound for it places the head in a position where it will not tie up the rest of the body, either on the backswing or in the act of hitting the ball. Whenever you see a leading golfer hit a ball, watch his head. You will find that he either starts his swing with his head cocked or else he turns it back for a few inches as the club goes back. And it won't make any difference whether he is "left-eyed" or "right-eyed."

Back in 1927 it happened that Joe Kirkwood and I were on the same ship going to St. Andrews for the British Open. The captain of the vessel was kind enough to rig up a driving net for us on the upper deck, and every day Joe and I would go up to hit a few balls. The practice was of no value, even with a gentle roll of the ship, but it did serve to prevent our hands becoming tender. But hammering balls into a net is dull business at best, and finally, Joe began to do some of his famous trick shots and, of course, I tried to follow him. Naturally, there were very few I could accomplish without more practice than we had time for.

But one series of shots which Joe introduced to me shed a good bit of light on this question of the position of the head. These shots were played with an iron. Three balls would be placed on the mat in line, and Joe would hit the first while looking directly behind him, the second while looking into the eye of an observer standing directly across the ball from him, and the third while looking in the direction in which the flag or the objective would lie. That looked fairly simple, after locating the first ball, so I had a go at it. After a few trials I could hit the first ball, looking down the deck away from the canvas, and the second looking at Joe standing at the other end of the mat, but the third, looking into the canvas in the direction of the flag, I could never hit, nor even make a respectable pass at it. With my chin to the front I found it impossible to turn my hips or to swing the club back at all. The most I could do was to lift the club up and back at the ball.

Alex Morrison, more than anyone else, I think, has harped upon the "chin-back" idea. I am convinced that it is sound for it places the head in a position where it will not tie up the rest of the body, either on the backswing or in the act of hitting the ball. Whenever you see a leading golfer hit a ball, watch his head. You will find that he either starts his swing with his head cocked or else he turns it back for a few inches as the club goes back. And it won't make any difference whether he is "left-eyed" or "right-eyed."

On Proper Position at the Top of the Swing

It is always best for the player to consider the golf stroke as one flowing and uninterrupted motion backward and forward from the position of address through the ball to the finish. This view is far more valuable than that which regards the swing as a series of distinct motions. Nevertheless there are a number of crucial points where proper or improper action may determine the ultimate success of the effort. An error here may be corrected there and the effect of the mistake avoided, but a proper start places one far along the road to a happy ending.

> The backswing is, of course, important
> because it is the means of placing the
> player in position to hit.

This is particularly true of the start of the downward or hitting stroke. The backswing is, of course, important because it is the means of placing the player in position to hit. But it is possible to reach a proper position in any number of ways, and corrections are more easily made when the motion is leisurely. Once started downward, the player launches himself upon his venture and right or wrong he must go through with it.

How Shaft Should Be Pointing.

Now there are a number of important things to be watched in the position at the top of the swing. It is possible to write many pages on this phase of the stroke. But the one feature which I have in mind now is one which the duffer ignores entirely and which has everything to do with the success of the stroke.

At the top of the swing the shaft of the club, which for the long shots is in a position approximately in a horizontal plane, should at the same time be pointing to a spot slightly to the right of the object at which the player is aiming. This can be found to be a uniform practice among the best professional golfers. It is the result of swinging the club back to the top rather than lifting it up, as so many beginners do.

Watch the Right Hand.

Now from this position it is important in what manner the club is started downward. The necessary elevation of the hands at the top of the swing draws the right elbow away from the ribs where it should have remained until the last possible moment. The elbow is not, however, lifted into the air like the wing of a wounded bird. The right forearm should point down almost vertically toward the ground, to be drawn away from the side only by what is necessary to accommodate a full swing of the club.

A good many players advance thus far with fair success. But the next step usually trips them. The almost irresistible impulse now, when all is in readiness to wallop the ball, is to allow the right hand too much freedom. Immediately that ubiquitous member, which has to be watched continually, whips the club over the right shoulder toward the front of the player, whence it must approach the ball from outside the line of flight. Whether a smothered hook or a bad slice results depends only upon whether the club face is shut or open when it reaches the ball. If anything like a decent shot results it may be ascribed to pure accident.

> The almost irresistible impulse now, when all is in readiness to wallop the ball, is to allow the right hand too much freedom.

The proper beginning from the position I have described is in the direction in which the grip end of the shaft is pointing. As the head end of the club is pointing slightly to the right of the objective aimed at, the grip end will be directed away from the vertical plane in which the ball rests. In other words, instead of immediately beginning to approach the line of flight as the downward stroke commences, the clubhead should be made to first drop away from that line.

The importance of this movement cannot be overestimated. The right elbow quickly drops back into place close to the side of the body and the player is in a compact position ready to deliver a blow squarely at the back of the ball. There is no possibility of cutting across the shot.

I regard Chick Evans' swing as a remarkable example of the importance of this movement which I have described. Chick violates one of the most commonly appreciated principles of a good golf swing in the way he takes his club back, lifting it almost vertically upward from the position of address. But he reaches a proper position, and when his club starts downward it drops away from the plane of the ball and sweeps through in a fine arc.

Reaching the proper position at the top and starting away correctly, it makes no difference in what way he progresses upward.

ON THE NEED FOR SOUND FUNDAMENTALS IN THE SWING

A ll golfing methods differ from each other in many particulars. Each good player presents an appearance so unlike any other that he can be recognized from great distances merely by the manner in which he swings his club. The inexperienced observer often fastens on to these differences, concludes that each man employs a radically different swing, and sets about modeling his form upon that of a player he will select. And that one he will ape faithfully and exactly to the last detail.

> It seems to me that a thorough understanding of these fundamentals of the stroke is the first thing at which the beginner should aim.

A closer study of the better players reveals the fact that while no two are alike, or even nearly so, still there are certain things both large and small which all of them do. Not only are we justified in regarding these unanimously accepted practices as sound, but it would seem that every golfer, large or small, fat or lean, would do well to adopt them as his own. The fact that almost every effective swing displays certain things in common with all the others is evidence enough that these things ought to be a part of every method.

Stroke Foundation Essential.

Indeed, these are about the only details of the stroke that the instructor is able to give to a rank beginner. These are the only things which he can tell him positively to do. The rest of the job consists of correcting faulty movements and in fitting together a stroke upon the proper foundation already supplied. But the stroke as a whole is not developed upon any set lines. The fundamentals must be observed, but there is great latitude allowed for accommodating individual needs.

> The fundamentals must be observed, but there is great latitude allowed for accommodating individual needs.

It seems to me that a thorough understanding of these fundamentals of the stroke is the first thing at which the beginner should aim. It might be said, of course, that there is a fundamentally correct swing from which everyone varies only slightly.

But that is not what I mean, for a thorough understanding of that sort of a swing and the ability to produce it are the two things that all of us are seeking and so few have ever attained. I have reference only to the obvious things which are easily seen and accomplished by the average inexperienced player, things that an ordinarily good player learns for himself and an expert never has to think about, but nevertheless points which can be noted by everyone at a great saving of time and trouble.

Sound Swing Leads to Success.

One of the great reasons for the consistency of the best players is the possession of a sound swing, by which we mean nothing more than a swing in which the successive positions are taken in accordance with accepted practice among expert players. It will be found that the man who departs far from what we call the orthodox, if he is even at times effective, is yet an erratic and unreliable player. He who starts in an unexciting position and commits no unwarranted extravagance is usually the more consistent player, because he places himself in positions and moves his club in paths from which and through which other successful players have found the going easier. All men are enough alike to make it safe to follow examples which have been proved effective by others.

> It will be found that the man who departs far from what we call the orthodox, if he is even at times effective, is yet an erratic and unreliable player.

In my next column I am going to try to point out a few things that I have observed to be a part of nearly every expert's method and to give some reasons why these things are important. I believe there are certain things which the beginner can well make up his mind to do if it kills him.

ON THE PROPER "HIP ACTION"

The proper handling of the hips is a very important factor in long driving. And because the average player either makes too little use of the hips or employs them incorrectly, I think there is a chance that some good may be done by an examination of the movements.

> Because the average player either makes too little use of the hips or employs them incorrectly, I think there is a chance that some good may be done by an examination of the movements.

In bringing the hips into play the golfer is attempting to utilize the powerful muscles of the back and leg, and while form and style count a great deal, still the only way to drive a ball a long way is to hit it hard. Good form simply is the means of eliminating waste and of exerting in a useful way a greater proportion of the physical strength which the player possesses.

In slow motion pictures we have an opportunity to see a lot of things which we can't see with the naked eye. But the trouble is that we can't see ourselves, either. Our effort should be to study the pictures, the positions, etc., and translate these in terms of "feel." We must have the conception of motion as well as a presentation of the successive positions.

Back Turned to Hole.

Almost every first-class golfer turns his hips quite freely away from the ball during the backswing. In nearly every case the back of the player will be presented squarely to the hole— that is the upper part of the back between the shoulders, for necessarily the hips turn less than the upper portions. There is a noticeable amount of twisting above the waist.

If this turn and twist are regarded, just as the wrist-cock, as a source of power, the problem is then to unwind in proper timing to deliver the maximum blow at the right instant. The expert golfer begins to unwind his hips at the beginning of his downswing. The turn back to the ball begins slowly, just as the downswing itself begins slowly, and the sudden powerful twist is reserved for hitting just as the wrist-cock is saved. It is important that the left hip should turn out of the way, but it is also important that the hips should not be twisted so quickly that the power of their position will be used up in the first part of the downward stroke.

Action of Left Knee.

The action of the left knee almost exactly parallels the correct wrist action. This knee bends forward and swings to the right during the backswing. During the downstroke it swings to the left but does not straighten immediately. It actually becomes straight just before impact as the final powerful twist of the hips takes place. It is this twist which straightens the leg and throws the kneecap back and gives the impression, so often stated, that the player is "hitting against the left leg." I don't like that expression, because it suggests that a resistance is interposed by the left side. This is a dangerous thing to encourage.

> It is this twist which straightens the leg and throws the kneecap back and gives the impression, so often stated, that the player is "hitting against the left leg."

As a matter of fact, there is no question that the long-hitters twist the hips through quite an arc and they actually do so with a great deal of effort. I don't know how to describe it better than to say it is a powerful wrench of the body.

I have the feeling when playing well that during the first part of the downstroke I am pulling against something. There really is nothing to pull against except the tension in my own muscles—there is another dangerous word, but there is no other that fits—set up by the effort of the stroke.

More or less rapidly this is overcome and finally wrists, body, arms, and legs all join to deliver their power simultaneously. The proper timing of these factors with each one prepared to the limit, is the real secret of long driving.

THE HIPS ARE PULLING AGAINST THE COCKED SHOULDERS.

ON PLAYING A
"SPARED" VS. "FULL" STROKE

Whether to spare a stronger club or force a weaker one is a decision which has to be made on almost every shot in golf. Except in playing off the tee there hardly ever arises a situation which does not hold at least two possibilities—two clubs and two kinds of shots which can be played—and the player who consistently chooses the easier of these two ways in the long run must gain a considerable advantage.

> Generally speaking, I think it is wise to play a full shot, or possibly a forced shot downwind, and a half or spared shot into the wind. With the wind behind, there can be but little reliance upon backspin.

The larger ball has made possibilities of this nature quite a bit greater. It has actually brought the game, particularly the iron-play, back closer to what it was years ago, when the half-iron shot was so important. With the larger ball there has reappeared the necessity for keeping the shot down when playing into any sort of a headwind. The small, heavy ball could be played with almost no regard to a moderate breeze. Its flight became slightly less, of course, but the matter of control and direction did not make a low-flying shot a necessity.

Besides this, quite aside from wind effect, it has been possible to play shots with the larger ball which could never be thought of when the smaller projectile was in use. There were shots which had to be stopped so quickly that the only possible method was to play a good full shot with a lofted club to throw the ball high into the air. The smaller ball was much harder to stop. Now a great number of these shots can be made half-shots with less lofted clubs. We have come back closer to the times when Johnny Ball could play nearly all of his shorter approaches with a mid-iron. The player now has a greater need for knowledge of the value and possibilities of a spared shot than he had for a number of years.

Generally speaking, I think it is wise to play a full shot, or possibly a forced shot downwind, and a half or spared shot into the wind. With the wind behind, there can be but little reliance upon backspin.

If the shot must be prevented from rolling, its elevation must do the work. When playing into the wind, any well-hit shot will stop. But the ball must be held relatively low in order to hold its direction. In these two instances the choice is practically forced. The spared shot cannot be played with a breeze behind unless the ground in front of the green is open and there is no necessity for quick stopping; the full shot, carrying high, cannot be relied upon in the face of any considerable breeze.

The spared shot cannot be played with a breeze behind unless the ground in front of the green is open and there is no necessity for quick stopping; the full shot, carrying high, cannot be relied upon in the face of any considerable breeze.

69

Without wind the choice becomes in many instances entirely optional. It is then merely a matter of the players' preference, and since a good many average golfers are afraid of a spared shot they favor the other kind. I doubt if even an expert ever has a day when he can play either shot with the same feeling of confidence. At least he is likely to favor one or the other according to the way he is swinging.

But a lack of confidence in the half-shot may cause a player to choose to take a full swing; it can never alter the fact that the half-shot in some instances is better to use. The average player ought to try to learn it.

Watch Out for the
Left Wrist

PRONATE

One of the things which would help the average golfer to understand is that there is very little pronation of the left wrist, or rotation of the left forearm in the correct golf swing; and that the effort to introduce either is about as harmful as anything that could be done.

Reasons for the contrary impression are not difficult to find. It is certainly sure that any position close to the halfway mark either going up or coming down exhibits the left hand presenting its back approximately square to the front, or very nearly at right angles to its position at address. It is not unnatural to assume that this is in great measure the result of pronation, and is itself alone responsible for "opening" and closing the face of the club.

So we commonly observe the average golfer beginning his backswing by a sudden pronation of the left wrist, turning the palm underneath, and directing the club in a very flat arc around his knees. In this manner he conceives himself to be opening the face of the club, when in actual fact, he is doing nothing more than removing all possibility of correct body movement. In a great majority of cases, this sort of action is accompanied by a left shoulder that comes around too high, and a movement of weight toward the left foot during the backswing.

In the downswing, too, this misconception leads to trouble, for conceiving that in order to reclose the face in the act

3 knuckles?

X

3 knuckles

...must be turned back over, the player
...side into such a tight place that it must
...o be a lot of talk about the "right hand
...ft" but it must be understood that this
...ter impact when everything has relaxed
...fort.

...portant in gripping the club to place the left
ha... ...extent on top of the shaft. How much, of
course, ...ary, but enough so that three knuckles of the
hand can be seen by the player as he looks down would not be
extreme. In this way, the usefulness and strength of the left
side and arm are assured.

The thing we want most in the backswing is ample and
correct body turn. Too many players make the mistake of attempting to turn the shoulders horizontally, without permit-
ting the natural dip of the left shoulder which would normally
occur as the body turns on an inclined axis. This, of course,
causes the head to move, and is a very bad mistake.

All this is only made worse by any amount of pronation of
the left wrist at the beginning of the backswing. Indeed, a
slight twist of the wrists in the opposite direction—supination
of the left—can very well be used to start the swing off right.

But the opening and closing of the face of the club are
amply cared for by the correct body movement. When the
player addresses the ball he squares his club to the hole, and
in his grip he determines the relation of his left hand to the
club face—the striking area. This relation, of course, remains
the same throughout the swing, so that in order to bring the
face back square to the ball the left hand must come back in
the same position. And in the correct swing the body
movement will ensure that it does so without a great deal of
manipulation.

HIP TURN

One of the most common reasons or excuses offered by the average golfer for a bad slice is that he "got his body in too soon." As any such idea as this is bound to discourage an ample use of the hips and back (exactly the point wherein I believe the average player is most remiss) and because in nine cases out of ten it is entirely wrong, I think a little consideration of the body movement in the downswing may be helpful.

Motion pictures of numbers of our best professionals disclose three common characteristics which are important to a discussion of this particular point. First, the hips begin to unwind, that is, to turn back toward the ball, even before the club has reached the end of its backward travel; second, the left heel returns to the ground very early in the downstroke while the hands are at shoulder-level or above; and third, the hips at impact have turned through their locations at address and at this point the lower part of the body fronts almost toward the hole.

Thus, it is impossible to escape the fact that the unwinding of the hips in the correct swing is very rapid indeed.

I have often observed precisely the same action in a baseball pitcher warming up close to the stands before a game. There is no doubt that the quick twist of the hips beginning the throwing movement supplies important momentum which increases both speed and endurance. If a pitcher were to eliminate his hip movement or retard it to such a degree that it would be useless he would be a very weary young man at the end of nine innings.

The momentum obtained by the golfer, when the unwinding of his hips leads the hitting movement, is no less important to him than to the pitcher. For one thing, it makes it possible for him to attain a much greater speed at impact with appreciably less effort.

I have tried many times, in testing this idea, to turn my hips too rapidly in hitting a full drive. I have found it impossible to do as long as I observed the rudiments of good form. Indeed, I have been able to trace a good many errors to a slowing down or stopping of the hip-turn too quickly.

The average golfer usually experiences trouble for one of two reasons. Either he omits the forward movement or shift of the hips which must precede and blend in with the beginning of the turn or he moves his whole body, including head and shoulders, in a sort of lunge at the ball. He cannot hope to do other than cut across the ball if he holds the greater portion of his weight upon his right leg or falls back upon it as he brings his club down.

In the correct swing, starting down, the hips should shift forward slightly before any noticeable unwinding takes place. I like Abe Mitchell's expression that "the player should move freely beneath himself." In other words, the head and shoulders should not accompany the hips in this initial movement.

I have often referred to the stretch which I feel up the left side and arm from hip to hand, the result of leading the downswing with the hip-turn. Now the hands drop almost vertically downward, starting the right shoulder moving below the left. From this point the swing is able to pass through the ball on a line approximately straight to the objective.

Handling the several movements in this way, as I have said, I have not found it possible to turn the hips too quickly.

Whenever a player "gets his body into the shot" in any way greatly different from this, he is wrong whether he does it "too soon" or not.

THE LEFT ARM
AT IMPACT

Almost all competent instructions of golf agree that hitting through with the left arm and left side is of first importance in striking a golf ball correctly. Whatever might have been the theories of other days, the slow-motion camera has now shown beyond any question that the straight left arm at impact is a characteristic common to all our great stylists.

But now that we are able to say what the left arm should do, we are up against the far more difficult problem of finding a way to make it do what it ought to. It is easy enough to say, "Keep the left arm straight." But the average golfer wants to know how he can do it.

Position at Impact.

I have attempted to stress many times the importance of starting the backswing mainly with the left side in order to encourage a full extension of that arm. This is the best means of straightening the arm from its relaxed condition at address. But many good players obtain satisfactory results without a perfect straightness of the left arm at the top of the swing. Of far greater importance is the behavior of this member in the act of striking the ball. It was my observation that most of the really bad shots played at Fresh Meadow were directly attributable to left arms, which collapsed in the act of hitting or otherwise failed to carry through.

Briefly stated, I think the most common cause of the collapse of the left arm at this time results from the left elbow, in one way or another, being forced in against the side of the body. Or stated another way, in order to hit through with the left side, the arm must be in such position that the elbow joint, rather than the outside, on the arm, is viewed as it hangs at the side.

Left Elbow Points.

Many players appear to fear that the clubhead will not catch up in time, consequently they attempt to throw or "cowtail" it in ahead of the hands—exactly the thing which causes the left arm to fold up and become entirely useless. I have seen a good instructor, upon taking charge of such a pupil, shock him almost out of his senses by telling him to try to hit the ball with the sole of his club. The only thing intended to be accomplished by such advice was to turn the left elbow away from the side, so that the left arm could carry through.

An examination of the grip used by expert golfers will show that in every instance the left hand is to some degree on top of the shaft. The effect of this also is to present the elbow somewhat toward the hole, and to prevent a clamping of the upper left arm against the side of the body. The left arm should work closely across the chest and front, but there must never be any suggestion of the player's "hugging himself" with it.

ELIMINATE THOSE
EXTRA MOVEMENTS

As has so often been said, the soundest golf swing is the simplest one, in which no unnecessary movement is made. The swing which introduces needless requirements of timing may at times be reasonably successful. But on those days which inevitably arrive when the timing is not so precise, such a swing must fail. In order to play consistent golf, what we should strive for is a swing which will work passably well on the bad days. Then the good days will take care of themselves.

One of the most common mistakes of this kind, which introduces a new and entirely unnecessary timing requirement into the swing, is the up and down movement of the head which one notices even in the swings of some very good golfers. The motion usually begins from a crouching position at address, whence the head moves upward during the backswing, downward as the club starts down, and upward again as the body stretches out in the effort of hitting. It is not difficult to see that these several movements add important complications to an action which already requires accurate timing, for particularly the last upward movement must be timed to accommodate the stretching of the left side in order to bring the clubhead against the ball. If the head moves up too quickly a topped shot will result, and if not quickly enough, the clubhead will hit the ground first.

Stay Down to the Ball.

One of the virtues which I like to see in any golfer is that of "staying down to the shot." The lift enforced by the straightening of the left leg is all right and develops power, but at the same time the arms and shoulders should be resisting this lift, aiding in the stretching of the left side. When the hands reach the lower part of the downswing there is a feeling of pushing down with the heel of the left hand.

Obviously the player cannot "stay down to the shot" if his head, arms, and shoulders are moving upward as he hits the ball. And it is equally obvious that these members must be moving upward if the player has gotten himself doubled up so that his position affords no room for his left side to stretch.

Stand Fairly Erect.

We often see a player take his stance, addressing the ball with left side entirely slack, his right hip higher than his left, and his right shoulder above the shoulder on the other side. The necessary complement of this picture is that the left arm should present a withered appearance, drawn up against the side of the body and showing an upward bend at the wrist.

This posture is the cause of most of the trouble. If the player would take a proper position at the start—one which would give the left side plenty of room to begin with—the temptation to crouch and straighten would be considerably lessened.

The real players all stand fairly erect with the left hip and shoulder noticeably higher than the right side. The left arm too is well extended, not entirely straight in the relaxed posture of address, but never giving the impression that it is being drawn up. The extension is always such that, although the body is erect, the left hand is so low that the bend of the wrist is downward.

This posture does not reproduce that which the player passes through in hitting the ball. To pose the latter sets up a great strain. But it approximates this position, and therefore assures plenty of space for the necessary action without the necessity for timing another set of movements to provide this space.

HANDLING HILLY LIES

In playing either a downhill or uphill lie the big problem is to handle the weight against the slope so that the ball can be struck as in any other golf shot. Admitting that the expert player adjusts himself almost instinctively to each situation or set of conditions, there is still a lot to be gained by knowing just what adjustment ought to be made.

Of the fairway lies and stances which are likely to be encountered in any line of golf, there remain two which can give a lot of trouble. I know of no convenient names which we can give to them, but all golfers will recognize the situations well enough. They are first a stance upon ground which slopes away from the ball toward the player and the other upon ground which slopes away from the player toward the ball. Ignoring the effect of any slope toward or away from the hole, the problem here is mainly one of controlling direction.

One of my correspondents writes that he has been advised in playing from stances of this kind to grip his club short or long as he was required to stand below or above the ball. Sometimes, of course, it is not entirely comfortable to grip the club at its full length when playing a ball which is considerably above the player's feet. In such a case it is a good practice to slide the hands down a bit, but this is only a beginning which will not of itself supply the necessary control. The usual troubles which the average player has when playing from sloping lies arise from two definite tendencies, one to slice when standing above the ball and the other, just as definite, to hook when standing below the ball. To learn control, the main idea should be to counteract these tendencies.

This is exactly the method which I have found to be most successful. When I am forced to take a stance on ground lower than that upon which the ball rests I open my stance a bit by advancing the right foot, point my left toe more nearly toward the hole, and play the ball well forward. And then in the stroking I am careful to exert a strong pull with the left side. In other words, when I want to hold the ball on a straight flight I cut across it slightly to counteract the tendency to hook.

When playing from a lie of the other kind, where I am standing above the ball, I attempt to counteract the slicing tendency by delaying the turn of my hips and by holding back a little with the left hand just before impact. These actions tend to whip the clubhead in front of the hands and if timed correctly will successfully counteract the slice which would normally result from such a position. In this case, too, the ball is played from a point about on line with the ball of the left foot.

Of course there are occasions when it is best to play these stances in a perfectly normal way, making allowance for either the slice or hook which will result. Particularly is this true when maximum length is desired and the player finds himself standing below the ball. After he learns exactly how much hook to allow for, he can use it to good advantage.

PITCHING FROM THE ROUGH

The average golfer loses more strokes around the greens than even his limited skill justifies. This does not always include the putting, for many players who score above 90, though they are not good putters, still manage well enough on the greens in comparison with the rest of their play. But a good number of the strokes they take are used up in getting up within holding distance after they have maneuvered the ball into pitching distance of the green.

In the short play, the shot which seems to give the most trouble is the very short approach from rough grass only a few feet or a few yards off the edge of the putting surface. From greater distances, when there is a chance to hit a little harder, the difficulty of obtaining reasonably good results is considerably less. But the shorter approach, especially if a keen green or declining slope complicates matters, requires real skill and a nicely gauged stroke. It offers a problem for even the most expert player.

The shot is difficult for two reasons. First, because it is almost impossible to know how much or how little resistance the long grass will offer, and second, because the grassy contact between club and ball and the softness of the stroke remove all chance of limiting the roll by the application of backspin.

The usual method of attempting a shot of this kind shows that this second reason is not always remembered, for the average golfer almost invariably tries to bring the ball out with a short, hacking stroke intended to produce a shot which will certainly reach the green but which will have enough spin to hold it near the hole. The result, either badly fluffed and still in the rough, or struck too hard, or half topped and over the green.

I think Harry Vardon was the most complete master of this stroke that I have ever seen. And Vardon always played it in the gentlest way imaginable, in contrast to the quick, jerky stroke employed by the average duffer. The long grass was seen as an added difficulty, but not one to be overcome by a hacking stroke.

This shot should always be played with a well lofted club, invariably a niblick, unless the ball should be actually teed up on the grass. This is done in order to get the ball free of the grass as quickly as possible. The stroke should be of ample length and unhurried and by all means the clubhead should be allowed to swing. I always like to think of the stroke as one which floats the clubhead against the ball in an effort to lob it gently onto the green without making any effort to limit its normal roll.

I do not mean to say that this method will suffice in every conceivable situation. It should be effective in 90 percent of the cases when playing from very short distances. At times when the hole happens to be cut very close to the edge of the green it may be necessary to adopt drastic measures. Sometimes a shot has to be played by cutting directly under the ball, employing a vicious stroke with the club laid back, or again one may have to trust to luck and try to bobble the ball through the intervening rough. But these are last resorts. It is time enough to worry about them when the ordinary situation has been mastered.

A Straight Line to
Straight Shots

Two very important things for the average golfer to remember are: First, that it does not help to throw the clubhead into the ball ahead of the hands, and second, that the right arm should not begin to rotate nor the right wrist begin to turn or "climb" over the left until after the ball has been struck. To attempt to get the clubhead in first or to roll the wrists are two favorite ways of "correcting" a slice. The only trouble is that they never work.

To hit a golf shot correctly the player must move toward the ball, not away from it, as his club gathers speed. At the instant of contact, he must be over the ball where he can perform consistently and accurately the job of hitting, and above all he must be in position to utilize the pull of his left side. He can't expect to get results by standing back and throwing the club at the ball.

The correct stroke causes the clubhead to approach the ball from inside the line of play. The factors which make this possible are the forward shift of the hips during the downstroke, maintaining a bend in the right arm which keeps the right elbow close to the side of the body, and the backhand nature of the stroke dominated by a strong pull from the left side. These are the factors which make it necessary or inevitable that at the instant of impact the hands should be on a line with or ahead of the clubhead and that the left hand should carry through the ball without beginning to turn.

The immediate cause of a slice is a contact between club and ball while the face of the club is directed to the right of the line upon which the club is moving. These conditions may be met when the clubhead is moving precisely along the line of intended flight, but when it is facing to the right of that line, or when the face is square to the line and the clubhead is moving across it toward the player's left. Unless the grip of the left hand has been relaxed enough to allow the club to turn in the fingers, the first set of conditions is rarely ever encountered. In correcting a tendency toward slicing, the problem is almost always to correct the direction of motion of the clubhead. *Yes, cutting across the ball*

Instead of making this correction the attempt to whip the clubhead in first only leads to more difficulty. The effort to hold everything back to allow the clubhead to get in front prevents the completion of the forward shift of the hips and assures that the stroke must cross the line of play from the outside, precisely the thing which it was sought to avoid.

The better idea is to concentrate upon holding the swing behind the line of flight passing through the ball. It is possible to groove a swing which hits down from the top, but not one which moves the clubhead outward.

When the weight stays back on the right foot and the forward shift is not completed, the stroke, as I have said, must come from the outside in. The result of such a stroke depends upon what the hands do to the face of the club. If the right hand rolls over the left before the ball is struck, the result must be a badly hooked or smothered shot.

In a sound golf stroke the back of the left hand is visible at the instant of impact to an observer standing immediately in front of the player. It is important that this hand should drive straight through the impact position in the effort to direct the head of the club precisely along the line of play. The turning

Left hand directs stroke

action, which begins to take place an appreciable space after contact, does so then because the player's muscles relax after the effort of hitting and because his swing has then reached the limit of motion which it can accommodate along the line of flight.

ON THE
PROPER DOWNSWING

One cannot help sympathizing with the poor fellow trying desperately to find some way of building up a sound swing, when he finds himself submerged in a sea of "do's" and "don'ts" with scarcely a chance of finding his way out. There can be no question that the chief reason golf is so mystifying to the beginner is to be found in the difficulty of expressing in a few words the simple fundamental necessities of form. There are numbers of people who devote enough thought, time, and hard practice to the game to make them reasonably good players if they could start out with an accurate conception of what they want to do. But in nearly every instance there is a confusion of ideas which makes intelligent progress impossible.

> There can be no question that the chief reason golf is so mystifying to the beginner is to be found in the difficulty of expressing in a few words the simple fundamental necessities of form.

One cannot select one motion or even one series of motions and say that this or these is or are fundamental. If a basic principle is to be found it must be broader than that. It must be

scribed procedure which can be
It must be something for the player
, rather than with his own body.

ntion or discovery to the theory of
ut. I don't even know that I agree
itting is indispensable to good golf,
the duffer is seeking a fundamental
practice and his development, he can-
solve never to permit his clubhead to
cross the pro̲j̲e̲c̲   ̲ of flight back of the ball. Whether he
will cross that line at or after impact depends entirely upon
the kind of shot he wants to play.

Almost every inferior player swings across the line of flight
from the outside to the inside. He is either a hooker or a
slicer, depending upon whether the club face is open or
closed at impact. One rarely finds a dub who stays at all times
inside the magic line.

In order to be helpful if possible let me suggest within this
limited space how I should go about learning to operate.

In the first place there are two points in the swing which
must be watched, two places where a misdirected move may
make a crossing of the magic line inevitable. One is at the moment when the club is started backward from the ball; the
other occurs as the club is started downward from the top. If a
man will practice starting upward and starting down with this
in mind I believe he can very soon learn to swing in the
proper groove.

In starting the club backward there is one thing which
may throw it outside. This is the right hand. If the player initi-
ates the motion by breaking his wrists, almost inevitably his
right hand and wrist will lift the club and carry it upward over
the shoulders.

The proper way to start the backswing is by rotating the
entire body, by turning the hips and shoulders upon a pivot,
at the same time bending the left knee and lifting the left foot
from the ground. I can think of no better way to make a start

than by "taking off" from the left foot, by rolling the weight toward the inside of that foot. The arms may move slightly, but only a few inches across the body. The hands, moving straight backward, drag the club away from the ball along the line of flight, then turn toward the inside.

This turning and swinging following naturally lead to a proper position at the top of the swing, with hands well back and the club pointing over the back of the neck to a point several yards to the right of the objective. The second danger point occurs here.

There are at least two things that can be done here to throw the clubhead beyond the line. To start with a pure turn of the body without throwing the hips forward is fatal because such a motion pulls the hands forward and this causes the clubhead to move more toward the player's rear. To swing outward and across the ball is then not only easy but inevitable. The same thing happens if the wrists are employed here to whip the club downward, as is so often advised.

There are three things which must be done to keep the club swinging inside of the line of flight. They are: First, the hips must be shifted quickly toward the front along the line of play, ever so slightly, yet definitely; second, the right elbow must return to the side of the body; and third, the hands must be moved or dropped a few inches backward and downward without straightening or starting to straighten the wrists. If this sort of a start is made the rest is easy.

I do not believe that the direction at impact should be actually from the inside out unless the player desires to produce a draw or hook. To play a straight shot I think the club should travel along the line of flight. But anything is better than playing always and helplessly across the ball. Sometimes to produce a fade or slice it must be done, but when the average player can't help doing it he is in a discouraging predicament.

On the Proper Method
of Shifting Weight

All this talk about transference of weight and the shifting of the weight forward upon the left foot during the downstroke is all fine enough and thoroughly sound provided it is understood just what sort of a shift is meant. Unfortunately I find that there are quite a few earnest and aspiring "average golfers" who are not entirely clear on this point. I am sure that there must be many others who cannot quite distinguish between the "shift," which they have been told is correct, from the "sway," which they have been told they must in no case permit.

Let me begin by saying that although I have in the past inclined toward a different view, it is now my definite opinion that there need be no shifting of weight from left foot to right during the backstroke. I have examined numbers of photographs of the very best players and I have been able to find no case in which such a shifting was perceptible. But there should occur during the hitting stroke a quite pronounced shift from the right to the left, a shift which does not follow the club or pass smoothly along coincident with its progress, but which is executed quickly and leads the arms and club all the way through.

The more expert players stand almost erect when addressing the ball. Rarely does one see a really first-class player bend or stoop over the ball. His body curves only very slightly and his weight is equally apportioned to each foot, and, if it is possible, evenly distributed over the area of each. In other words, he stands neither upon his heels nor upon his toes. From this position the proper body action is purely a turn or pivot with no shifting or sway whatever.

> I am sure that there must be many others who cannot quite distinguish between the "shift," which they have been told is correct, from the "sway," which they have been told they must in no case permit.

The downswing or hitting stroke presents another picture. There is a shift here, but there is no sway, and the difference is what the average golfer wants to understand. It is this: The weight shift which is proper is a shift of the hips—a lateral movement of the middle part of the body which does not alter the position of the head and shoulders: The sway, which is entirely improper, is a forward motion of the entire body, which sends the head and shoulders forward too, and tends to upset the player's balance.

There are two common methods of handling the weight improperly. The more damage is caused by settling most of the weight upon the left foot at the top of the swing. A beginner nearly always possesses a liking for this. Although sometimes we may overlook the root of the trouble, the result is a familiar sight. The effort of hitting always throws the weight violently back upon the right foot. The player falls away from the ball, his left foot flies up into the air and his balance is completely lost. The other method, too, we have often seen, where in the backswing the player draws his entire body backward and finds himself poised at the top with his entire weight upon his right foot and his left leg perfectly straight. This kind of a beginning ends in a despairing lunge at the ball, which usually carries it nowhere.

If we but examine the styles of different golfers, even with the naked eye, it is easy enough to tell whether the weight transference has been a sway or a shift. One characteristic of the proper body action, that is to say, the shift, is that the left leg is straight at and after impact. If you want to know why this is, you have only to look at the time, which marks the left side of the body. It has been lengthened, without lifting the head, by holding the shoulder back while the left hip goes forward. The characteristic of the sway, located again in the left leg, is a decided bend of the left knee in this same area. The entire weight of the body has been thrown forward. The shoulders coming forward also prevent the straightening of the left leg, and either the knee bends more or the player falls flat upon his face. The position I am trying to describe was perfectly illustrated by a photograph of Leon Erroll's trick knee in last March's *American Golfer*. If you saw that and remembered it, you'd know what I mean.

> One characteristic of the proper body action, that is to say, the shift, is that the left leg is straight at and after impact.

There are people who sway a little bit and get away with it. Tommy Armour is one, Joe Turnesa is another. Both are great golfers and both are led to sway because they hug the club in so tightly on the backswing. But Armour's is the more reliable variation, because, although he finishes with practically all his weight upon the left leg, he still manages to keep it straight, whereas Turnesa allows a perceptible bend in the knee.

Run-up Shot

One day last week I was playing a round with Frank Ball, professional at East Lake. On the thirteenth hole Frank's second shot left his ball some fifteen or twenty yards off the putting surface of the winter green. The fairway in front of this green is none too good, being allowed to grow up in rough when the summer green is in play, and since the hole had been cut very close to the near edge of the green, I was interested to see how Frank would play the shot.

> Most good players, I think, recognize
> the desirability of all these features in a
> shot of this kind, but few of them attack
> the problem in this way.

"Here's one I learned from Hagen," he announced, proceeding then to play a nice run-up which held its course remarkably well over the uneven ground, and finished quite close to the hole. As he played the shot the imitation of Hagen's style was evident, but the method was one which, though I had seen it many times, I had never noted as unusual.

The peculiarity of the stroke was the taut left forearm and almost rigid left wrist. The club was taken back with almost no aid from the wrists, and swung through the ball largely by

means of the arms and shoulders. There was very little opening of the club face on the backswing, and the ball, played farther back than usual, was simply batted along the ground.
The contact between the club and the ball had none of the
sharp, ringing quality that is characteristic of a shot which is
played with active wrists.

Watch Condition of Turf.

The chief difficulty involved in any run-up shot is to strike
the ball in such a way that neither its direction nor the length
of its roll will be greatly affected by inconsistencies in the
earth or turf. Many a pitch and run has been spoiled by striking in a place where the ground is softer or when the grass is
heavier than was expected.

Hagen's method overcomes this difficulty admirably. The
sweeping character of the blow, flattening as it does the arc of
the short flight of the ball and wholly eliminating any chance
of backspin, brings the ball to earth, nothing to hinder
its running freely. It will hold its line over obstacles which
would seriously affect a ball hit with even a very slight cut or
backspin.

Seek Simplicity in Shots.

Most good players, I think, recognize the desirability of all
these features in a shot of this kind, but few of them attack the
problem in this way. The usual method involves the use of a
club with very little loft, or, what amounts to the same thing,
hooding the face of the mashie or spade until the angle of its
face about equals that of a mid-iron This latter club, or a little
sawed-off cleek, which I have carried for several years, are my
favorites for this shot, for with them the stroke becomes little
more than an elongated putt. The straight face of the club

will keep the ball rolling without the necessity of extraordinary effort on my part.

The fact that the use of a straighter club eliminates some mechanical complications would recommend the use of such a club to the vast majority of golfers, for simplicity is above all what they should seek. But the Hagen method, pendulum-like in its action, would likely enable its user to maintain a greater accuracy in direction. That there is less opening of the club face on the backswing makes it easier to hit the shot straight for the objective.

ON A LONGER BACKSWING
FOR THE CHIP SHOT

B illy Burke says that he deems it important in playing chip shots to be certain to swing the club back far enough. The Open champion cites his own experience and declares that in starting a round he tries to make certain of an ample backswing when making his first few chips. After he strikes the first two or three correctly he knows he can go on doing it.

> In my opinion there has been entirely too much attention given to the conception that the length of the shot must be regulated by the length of the backswing, an idea which was advanced in an effort to insist upon always retaining the crisp, decisive quality of the hit.

There are at least two lessons in these words of Bill's; the first, the long backswing, is always timely, particularly when golfers begin to talk of overswinging and of the greater accuracy to be obtained from a more "compact" style; the second, equally important, stresses the importance in golf of "getting off on the right foot."

I might say that the first lesson particularly appeals to me because it embodies my own pet idea that most of our short shots, pitches, chips, and whatnots are spoiled by a backswing that is not long enough. The temptation always as we near the hole is to make the backswing too short and too fast, with the result that all rhythm and control is made to vanish. In my opinion there has been entirely too much attention given to the conception that the length of the shot must be regulated by the length of the backswing, an idea which was advanced in an effort to insist upon always retaining the crisp, decisive quality of the hit. Every shot should be firmly struck; the importance of that must not be overlooked, but in striving to assure this we must not be led to the absurd conclusion that we must come from a hundred yards down to fifty simply by cutting the backswing in half and expending a proportionate amount of effort in the half arc.

As a matter of fact, I doubt if it would be possible to notice any great difference in length between the swing which an expert would use for a pitch of a hundred yards and that which he would employ for a shot of sixty yards. The chief difference is that in playing the shorter shot he expends less effort. The contact is kept crisp and clean but the acceleration becomes more gradual. The ample backswing certainly is more pleasing to the eye, and it overcomes to a great extent any tendency to hurry the stroke. We all know how difficult it is to play the little shots smoothly and without yielding to the temptation to look up at the hole before the ball starts on its way.

The whole idea, it seems to me, is to encourage the player to swing the clubhead. The longer backswing gives the player a feeling of freedom and ease which extends even to his state of mind and relieves a good bit of his anxiety over the success of the stroke.

THERE'S A REASON FOR ALL THOSE CLUBS

The thing of first importance in golf is to swing the club correctly. But there is always the choice of club and method to be made by which the chances of success can be immeasurably increased or diminished. Even the most expert golfer is, after all, entirely human. Considering the wide gulf which separates him from the average golfer, it is surprising how far from perfection the very best human performer really is. No matter how good a player may become, judged by the standards which we know today, it will always be important for him to weigh the possibilities of each situation and to choose the simplest way of meeting it.

The mechanical side of the game is the thing which should be simplified. The possibility of obtaining carefully matched sets of clubs, covering with very small differences the entire change of loft, has unquestionably made the game easier.

Simpler to Change Clubs.

A range of shots which had to be played twenty years ago with one club and three variations of method are now played with three clubs and no variation. And it has been found to be a far simpler matter to change a club than a swing.

The value of these additional clubs has been readily

appreciated by the average golfer in his play through the green. He no longer needs to and no longer attempts to shorten the range of a club by cutting the shot or shortening the swing except within very narrow limits. He has a club for almost every distance and, in the long game, he uses them.

But it has been my observation that a further possible simplification on the mechanical side has been neglected, for it is not generally recognized that the wider assortment of implements can be helpful in the short game as well. Just as the varying lofts can be made to take care of the different ranges with little alteration in the swing, so they can also be useful in adjusting the relation of pitch to roll in the very short approaches without the need for the clever little cuts and delicate backspin shots which bring so much grief.

This is so obvious that it sounds foolish. Yet it is amazing how many players attempt to play every kind of chip or shot approach with one club. You probably know the man well who, as soon as he sees his ball near the green, straightway hauls from his bag some sort of sawed-off mashie or mid-iron. He has already made up his mind to use that club because he has always done so and he will use it no matter what kind of lie he may have or where the hole may be cut.

Pitch to Edge of Green.

Some sort of cleek or run-up club with a short shaft and little loft can be very useful from just off the edge of the green. A club of much loft is uncertain in such a case. The shot to be played is very close to a putt, with only the necessity for lofting the ball over a foot or two of longer grass. But as the ball moves away from the edge of the green and the hole comes closer to that edge, the shot becomes an entirely different proposition.

Except in unusual circumstances, it is always better to pitch to the edge of the green, over the intervening area, which is never as smooth as the putting surface, and it is also better to play every such shot with the same straightforward stroke, without attempting any sort of cut or backspin. This, of course, can almost always be done by changing to a more and more lofted club as the pitch becomes longer and the roll shorter.

I use anything from a three-iron down to a niblick for shots which could properly be called chip shots. Often when playing to a keen downhill slope it will be surer to pitch with a niblick over even a few feet of intervening space than to run the ball through it. And it is always simpler to play a normal shot with a lofted club, allowing for a normal roll, than to attempt a backspin shot with a club of less loft.

Relaxed Putting
Leads to Good Results

It is characteristic of the methods of all fine putters that the blade, or head, of the club travels in a very flat arc. In no case does it rise abruptly either on the backswing or after the ball has been struck, but on both sides of the ball it holds to a course relatively close to the ground. It may be argued that good putting requires a great deal more than accurate striking of the ball, but there is no room for argument that accurate striking is not the first necessity because it affords the means of translating what the eye sees and the mind directs.

Hitting the ball even ever so slightly on the upstroke is no less a fault on or near the putting green than elsewhere through the fairway. Though it is more difficult to detect in the shorter strokes, there is here the same transference of weight from the right leg to the left which is so noticeable in the long iron play of the better players. Often the even flow forward is not accompanied by a motion which even a high-speed camera could detect, and this has led some to advise that the body should be held motionless in putting. My belief is quite contrary to this, being, briefly, that complete relaxation and ease of motion is necessary to the accomplishment of a rhythmic stroke of any length from the shortest putt to a full drive.

Body Must Cooperate.

One cannot start out with the intention of making any stroke with the hands alone or with the arms alone or with anything else alone and hope to swing the club easily and with a smooth rhythm. The effort to exclude any part or parts of the body from the action, to hold any part motionless, must set up a strain which will oppose the ease of movement which is so necessary.

In putting, if the club is swung from the left wrist as a hinge it is obvious that the clubhead must rise abruptly after striking the ball. Obviously, too, it will do the same if the left arm is braced and stopped dead at this point. And if the blade of the putter should begin to rise a moment too soon it will be moving upward when it strikes the ball. In order to cause the clubhead to follow a flatter arc and to sweep the ball along the green the left wrist must continue its motion. And as in every other stroke, better direction and more accurate striking is assured by carrying the left hand on through toward the hole without pulling it in or turning it over. As in every other stroke, there must be no holding back of the weight upon the right leg. The player is not using any particular part or parts of his anatomical structure, he is using it all, and it should all move together.

Sense Body Movement.

Whenever I argue this point I am met with the answer that no photograph of myself discloses any body movement when making a putt of six or eight feet of the presumably holeable length. I agree that there is no movement which can be measured against a background, but there is all the same—when I am putting well—enough to register upon my own senses. I make no effort to bring about this movement when making a short putt. It is permitted rather than forced, and it is valuable mainly because it gives a comforting assurance of complete relaxation.

When the rhythm of the stroke becomes difficult to catch I find that it helps to increase the bend of the knees and at the waist, and to lower the left shoulder when addressing the ball. In this way the fixing of the weight upon the right leg is effectively discouraged and it becomes easier to sweep the clubhead through close to the ground.

Swing, Don't Hit

In most cases when a person indulges in any intention to "hit" the ball, misfortune results, especially when, as so often happens, a player has made up his mind to "knock the cover off" the pesky thing. Hard hitting is necessary for distance, but rarely does any golfer find himself so perfectly in tune that he can exert his ultimate strength while retaining sufficient control. In almost every case the effort to gain ten yards results in the loss of twenty—or more.

Long driving is of inestimable benefit. In tournament play the man who can outdrive his opponent consistently and decisively enjoys a tremendous advantage, for playing two clubs shorter than his opponent on every second shot means that he can consistently equal a fine shot by his opponent with only an ordinary effort of his own. But he must get his length without straining. He must get it while still swinging, without having to "hit."

"Swing, don't hit" is the slogan of almost every first-class instructor. But how hard it is to resist the temptation to put just a little bit more into it. And when that temptation is yielded to, it means too much right hand and a blow that is delivered too soon. The right hand must be used, of course, for it would be silly to discard any source of power in a game that is necessarily a two-handed affair, but the effort to hit hard invariably causes the right hand to beat down the left. And so one source of power is given up for the sake of another, when both, properly coordinated, could have been used.

Recent tests with some electrical contrivance for measuring instantaneous velocities has shown that a light club can be swung with greater speed than a heavy one, and hence should drive a golf ball a greater distance. Experiments of some of the leading pros have developed the same fact—that they could gain appreciably greater length with a lighter club. But unfortunately direction and control count as well, and even distance depends upon the player's ability to strike an accurate well-timed blow. A golf club should never be too heavy to be handled easily, nor should it be so light that it will encourage a too-rapid, ill-timed swing. Often a player finds that a lighter club works surprisingly well for a while, but soon he discovers that he is swinging faster and faster until at last he becomes unable to hit a straight shot. The very light club for speed works well enough but it has to have enough weight to slow down the swing to a point where it can be controlled.

I should like every golfer or would-be golfer to take himself out upon a practice tee overlooking a polo field or similar piece of ground, marked off with white lines to indicate a sufficient number of yards. And then let him drive a number of balls hit both hard and comfortably so that a comparison may be made. And then let him decide if the great effort he makes when he goes out for one is really worthwhile. My guess is that on the average the drives he has really swung at will be longer, and I know they will be straighter.

Use Spin to Your Advantage

It is undoubtedly true that a vast number of golf shots are missed and strokes wasted by players of fair club-swinging ability because they have not a complete and correct understanding of the behavior to be expected of a golf ball when struck in certain ways. Time and again I have seen men hit shots to their entire satisfaction and be genuinely surprised by the action of the ball. Shots which they expected to stop quickly may go bounding over the green, and those which they expected to roll drop dead where they hit. And often because they intended to play a certain kind of shot but did not know how to strike the ball in order to produce the result which they had pictured.

A player of long experience and an understanding of these things, standing behind a shot, is able to tell by the flight of the ball whether it has any spin on it and if it will stop quickly or roll upon striking the ground. In turn, he knows the kind of a blow which he must deliver in order to produce the result desired and he senses the instant his club hits the ball whether or not he has performed the job correctly.

Understanding of Spin.

The effect of spin upon the flight of a golf ball is one of the most important things to be understood by any golfer. For it is an understanding which will enable him to overcome many difficulties before which he would otherwise be help-less, no matter how well he could swing a club.

For example: In driving into a head wind the chief thing wanted is length, and there is no need for the meticulous ac-curacy which would be required in playing a shot to the green. So the ball must be struck in a way which will give it the maximum carrying power. It must fly in an arched trajectory, so that it will always be boring its way forward.

The usual inclination in such circumstances is to hit the ball down in an effort to keep it low, but the man who tries this is usually surprised to find that although his tee shot may start low, toward the end of its flight it will begin to climb on the breeze and ultimately drop almost vertically and lifelessly to the ground. The downward blow which he has delivered has imparted a backspin or underspin which has produced this kind of flight. In such circumstances he should do exactly what he thinks is wrong. He should attempt to hit the ball squarely in the back and impart no spin whatever in it. A ball struck in this way may fly a bit higher in the early part of its travel, but it will strike the ground at an angle, with still plenty of roll left in it.

Shot to Green Needs Control.

But when we move down to the second shot—the shot to the green—the problem becomes entirely different. In this case the shot must be controlled, the distance must be exactly right, neither too much nor too little, and the direction must be accurate. In most instances it will be best to drop the ball lifeless on the ground and the flight which climbs or "peaks" toward the finish is the thing which is wanted.

So here we want backspin and in order to get it we must hit the ball down. At the beginning of its flight it is kept low by two factors. First, the straighter face of the club selected, which should be a bit more powerful than is actually needed; and second, the downward component of the striking force which produces the backspin. A ball struck in this way will fly relatively low at first, but it will climb into the wind and drop almost dead.

When the experienced player sees a ball flying high, but which nonetheless begins to come down rapidly, he knows that it will roll a considerable distance after it strikes the ground, but he will know also that a shot flying somewhat lower which seems to hang in the air and hover above the ground before it falls will stop almost dead where it drops. The first has been struck a "flatter" blow with practically no backspin imparted, while the second has been struck downward and has plenty of spin on it.

ADJUSTING THE STANCE TO HOOK OR SLICE

It is a fine thing for the golfer always to remember what he can do with his feet. Many times a tendency to hook or slice can be corrected by an intelligent adjustment of the stance, or if the player has advanced far enough to attempt such things, he can in the same way bring off a pull or a fade at will. It is not so much that the altered position directly affects the stroke, but that variations are induced when the player places himself in positions most encouraging to them.

> To assume a closed stance position the player pulls his right foot back away from the ball so that it rests several inches behind the line drawn through his left foot parallel to the line of flight.

The closed stance is regarded as the hooking stance, and the open stance as more likely to produce a fade or slice. The reasons are obvious. To assume a closed stance position the player pulls his right foot back away from the ball so that it rests several inches behind the line drawn through his left foot parallel to the line of flight. This accomplishes two things. First, it encourages a round flat swing with a free turn away from the ball, and second, it sets up a certain amount of

> The open stance, on the other hand,
> is not a position of power, but rather
> of control.

resistance in the left side at about the time of impact. Address-ing the ball in this position encourages the player to hit out-ward at the ball, and when he exaggerates the maneuver he has the feeling that he takes the ball upon the club face and swings it around to the left.

Closed Stance for Long Driving.

The closed stance is essentially the long-driving stance. I always use it when I want a little extra distance with the driver or brassie. When I employ it I am morally certain that I can hit as hard as I like without fear of cutting the shot into a right-hand bunker. Francis Ouimet stands in this way for al-most every shot with the wooden clubs. When Francis strays from the line his error is almost always on the hooking side caused by too much resistance by the left side of his body.

The open stance, on the other hand, is not a position of power, but rather of control. With the right foot advanced the player stands more directly over the ball and he has much more difficulty in turning his hips and shoulders during the back stroke. From this position he cannot easily accomplish a flat swing, hence he is apt to be more upright. The open stance advocate will be more likely to slice than to hook and will likely play most of his iron shots with a slight left to right drift. In the open position the player faces more toward the hole. Even at address his left hip is moved backward out of the way of the path of his hands, and at the time the right side is advanced so that it becomes an impediment to a round, sweeping swing. These two factors encourage cutting across the ball, which is a characteristic of the players who use this stance.

> The open stance advocate will be more likely to slice than to hook and will likely play most of his iron shots with a slight left to right drift.

Stance Has Many Changes.

It so happens that to cut a drive is one of the worst things possible, while to cut a pitch is nearly always desirable. Making allowance then for the irregularities of the ground which might produce variations, the stance undergoes a transformation from the teeing ground to the putting green. In playing the big shots, the driver, brassie, and long irons, I like to see the player stand with his right foot slightly back of or at least on line with his left, and for the shorter irons and pitches use an open stance.

J.H. Taylor uses probably the widest open stance in the world, and while Taylor's feet are never on line he widens the opening as he nears the green. I have seen him play a pitch shot when he was facing almost directly at the objective. I do not know that Taylor was ever noted as a long driver. Certainly he is not one now, and I think his open driving stance indicates that he never was, but he is a marvelously accurate player with every club, especially the mashie. Strangely enough, even with his very open stance he manages a moderately flat swing, but it is the acme of compactness and firmness.

ON MAKING THE
WARNER BROTHERS FILMS

R ecently some comment has appeared in the papers to the effect that ultra high-speed motion pictures made by the Jenkins Laboratories of Washington have revealed certain things about the golf swing which made it evident that the pros had been teaching wrong for years. The swings of Vardon, Miss Wethered, and myself were filmed and the results were illuminating, but I do not think it is quite fair to the numbers of excellent teachers in America today to say that they have been shown to be mistaken. I think it is better and more accurate to say that the pictures have actually demonstrated things which before were only suspected.

> When I first saw a slow-motion shot of
> my golf swing—that was a long time
> ago—I didn't believe it, just as more
> recently I didn't believe it when I first
> heard my voice in the talkies.

These P.G.A. pictures ought to be a marvelous contribution to golf. Photographed at the rate of thirty-two hundred pictures per second, they represent by far the fastest (camera speed) or slowest (projection speed) ever attained. For the trained and capable student of the game they should prove of great value. When the observer knows what he wants to see, these pictures afford him the opportunity to actually study the motion. In the hands of the pros—men who are capable of interpreting them—they are indirectly going to be of value to the average golfer, and it is particularly gratifying that the pictures of all three players portray the same fundamental movements. I don't believe the pictures would have been of much value if it had been found that the three models selected were all different. Indeed, it is hard to imagine a more confusing occurrence.

Of course it is always interesting to see one's own swing as others see it. When I first saw a slow-motion shot of my golf swing—that was a long time ago—I didn't believe it, just as more recently I didn't believe it when I first heard my voice in the talkies. In the first pictures, I didn't believe that the portrayal of my hip action was at all correct. Since then, of course, I have seen the same thing numbers of times, in my own swing and in pictures of other people until I know now that it is really true. I think, now that we have had years of slow-motion study, almost every first-class golfer knows well enough how he hits the ball. The guess has been removed.

> But even slow-motion pictures need interpretation. The one great difficulty from the standpoint of the average golfer has been in separating the consciously controlled movements from those that are purely instinctive.

But even slow-motion pictures need interpretation. The one great difficulty from the standpoint of the average golfer has been in separating the consciously controlled movements from those that are purely instinctive. And this is just where the pro or interpreter comes in. It is his job to point out the things which ought to be watched, the things which are subject to control. These are the important fundamentals. If these are learned correctly the other movements follow naturally.

Many people have asked me if I have learned anything from the making of the series of pictures upon which I am now working. I don't think that that was to be expected, because I have had the opportunity for years to see my swing in slow motion. I have learned a great deal about the swing since I began writing about it some four years ago and began to analyze the hitting more critically than I had done before. Neither the P.G.A. pictures nor the ones which I am now making have shown me anything new. All they have done has been to confirm over and over again things that I felt all along I was doing or had seen in previous pictures. The one really illuminating thing out here in Hollywood has been that with the almost endless photographing I have had a chance to select shots that I know are good because of results and to compare them with the bad ones. By registering results it is possible to tell without guessing what caused a certain shot to go off line.

One thing, though, which I have not had at my command before has been exceedingly interesting. Even a slow-motion picture moves along at a speed which makes a study of position possible only to the trained eye. Although slow, it is still a representation of motion, and it is of course impossible for a golfer to pose the various attitudes through which he proceeds in hitting a ball. But by taking a high-speed shot and reprinting one frame which it is desired to examine, the motion can be stopped at any point for as long as is necessary. When it has been studied the motion is resumed as though nothing had happened. Thus we may see the swing flow into any position, hold it there, and when we have seen enough, allow it to pass on. This is of immense value when we are focusing on one detail or one phase of the stroke.

On Exaggerating a Useful Golf Tip

It is an exceedingly difficult proposition to put into words one's conception of how a golf ball ought to be hit. It is equally hard for a person to gain a fair impression by reading a description, however accurate and authoritative it may be. The first really practical method of teaching is of course personal instruction, where both the teacher and the pupil have a club in hand, and one can illustrate and correct, the other repeat and swear.

The great trouble with a bald description of the stroke without actual illustration is that there is almost always made an exaggerated impression of the movement sought to be described. Everything can be overdone, and usually is when one's attention is directed toward it. If one is told that a certain thing should be watched and a certain motion made, the determination to do just that almost always results in exaggeration, or in having something else undone. To strike a golf ball correctly requires a highly accurate blow. Considering this, it must be understood that variations in any part of the stroke cannot be very wide. Certain actions appear decided when attention is focused upon them, and many are stressed unduly in order to emphasize their value. But to read with profit, allowance must be made for exaggeration and the inclination to follow advice, although it be before one's eyes in black and white, must be tempered with reason.

A Case in Point.

I can still recall the first time I tried to reconstruct a golf shot from a written description. I was an awkward youngster, just in high school but tremendously interested in golf, when I read a most interesting article by Harry Vardon. In it Vardon at some length had painstakingly described what was then called the "push shot." Vardon himself had made the shot famous, and I had read all about the marvels he had accomplished with it. I concluded immediately that I must learn, so off I set with a hatful of old balls to the practice tee at East Lake.

> The first really practical method of teaching is of course personal instruction, where both the teacher and the pupil have a club in hand, and one can illustrate and correct, the other repeat and swear

I could have saved myself a lot of trouble and my wrists a lot of punishment if I had consulted Stewart Maiden before I started work. But Stewart was already giving someone a lesson. So I picked out a nice spot where there was plenty of turf to dig up, scattered out the balls, selected a mid-iron and began trying to go through the motions as I fancied Vardon had described.

The "push shot" was intended to be played with a short backswing and a vigorous punch downward through the ball. The wrist action was to be restricted, or so I gathered from the article. The purpose of the stroke was to send the ball off on a low trajectory but with a backspin which would cause it to stop quickly about the second or third hop.

I am sure my efforts must have been funny, for I dug up

turf with the energy of a ditchdigger working at 25 cents a spadeful. I obtained the low trajectory without much trouble, because I half topped almost every shot, but the backspin eluded me. When finally I looked around and saw Stewart grinning I gave up learning the push shot.

Overemphasis Gives Wrong Lead.

My mistake was exactly that of the others who read something that sounds well yet will not work in their particular case—I exaggerated everything Vardon wrote. I remember that he advised a forward swaying of the body to enable the player to hit a sharply descending blow. He probably meant a sway of an inch or so and an angle of contact of ten to fifteen degrees. I was swaying at least three inches and the angle was nearer forty-five degrees.

> Watch any good player play a fading shot intentionally—ask him to do it. Then see if your eye can detect the variation he makes in order to produce the fade.

Watch any good player play a fading shot intentionally—ask him to do it. Then see if your eye can detect the variation he makes in order to produce the fade. It will be largely your imagination if you can. Yet if you were told how to do it and you attempted to follow literally the explanation, you would likely produce something entirely unlike your normal swing. And it would not be all your fault either, for your teacher would be up against the problem of finding words to stress certain points of the stroke without overemphasis and without exaggerating the variation desired.

ON PLAYING IN
RAIN AND BAD CONDITIONS

Although conditions of ground and weather do objectively affect the playing of golf, a great deal of the adverse effect is caused by the state of the player's mind. A hard wind or a heavy rain inspires in the player a feeling of combativeness or of desperation, and prevents him from going about his business in an equable frame of mind. He is tempted to strive to do a little bit more than he can—to hit a little harder, or to exercise nicer control. It is only after a lot of experience that one learns that best results are reached by refusing to regard the elements except as a circumstance to be considered in deciding upon the character and direction of the shot. If we regard them as definite contrary forces which must be overcome, they in reality become very powerful enemies.

> A hard wind or a heavy rain inspires in the player a feeling of combativeness or of desperation, and prevents him from going about his business in an equable frame of mind.

Walter Hagen last year furnished an outstanding example of what can be done by keeping and using one's head. It was in the second round of the Open championship at Olympia

Fields. Walter had gone out in 40 and played the tenth hole only of the incoming nine when he was overtaken by a veritable torrent of rain, accompanied by some amount of wind. I had finished only a short while before the storm broke and had reached the shelter of the clubhouse in time. Looking out from my window I could scarcely see through the rain to the tenth tee, not over 100 yards away. I naturally thought of Hagen's situation. Out in 40, it seemed unlikely that he could better that figure coming home. An 80 for the round would mean substantially elimination.

Greens Play in Rain Easier.

But Hagen did on that nine what no golfer in the world can do as well as he. He shut his eyes and his mind to the rain and wind. He thought of only one thing—of getting the ball into the cup—and came back in 33. I saw him afterward and asked him in wonder how he had been able to accomplish the remarkable score. He apparently wasn't quite sure himself—"Just played golf," which after all is a pretty fair explanation.

When there is only rain to contend with without wind or unusual cold, the difficulty is almost wholly of the players' own making. Aside from slippery grips and water which trickles icily down one's neck there is no reason why even a heavy rain, unless it inundates the course, should offer any insurmountable problem. The wet turf takes a few yards off the drive, but the play around the greens is made correspondingly more simple. Often it is a joy to putt on a soaked green where every putt may be struck boldly for the hole.

Bad Conditions Sometimes Help.

In 1922 at the Brookline championship during the second qualifying round there came a deluge. When I reached the first green the whole surface was covered with water and it was necessary to putt with a mashie. Bernard Darwin, who came over that year as a member of the British team, had returned to the clubhouse confident that the day's play would be thrown out. Playing fourteen holes in the rain, I was very pleased with a 72, a stroke better than I had accomplished the day before in the glorious sunshine. But Jesse Guilford, playing immediately behind me, turned in a 70 and Chick Evans, finishing some time ahead and hence playing the full round in the worst of the rain, finished in 74. The fact that all three of us had improved noticeably upon the scores of the day before and there were many others who did likewise, is evidence enough that the downpour was not a serious handicap.

Many players who have a right to be rated above the average are quite happy with the game as long as conditions remain pleasant and normal. But a little wind or a drop or two of rain immediately throws them into such a panic that they can by no means do themselves justice. Sometimes their dejection reaches the extent of complaint and protest against a situation which they can in no wise alter. It is, of course, reasonable to expect that unfavorable weather will add a few strokes to the score in the end but there is no reason to allow a call of a dozen or more.

THOUGHTS ON THE
MENTAL SIDE

O lin Dutra in a recent interview has made some interesting observations upon the psychological side of competitive golf, telling of the difficulties on the mental side of trying to break through in important competition against the big names of professional golf. Dutra has had a remarkable season, producing some of the most amazing scoring feats that the game has seen. He does not believe that he is a much better shot-maker today than he was three years ago, and he attributes his improved scoring in competition to a change in his mental attitude.

Golf is certainly "an 'umbling game," as has so often been said, and it is a game which no reasonable man in his right mind would approach with complete assurance. The more golf one plays, the better he comes to realize that he cannot keep it under his thumb. Blind and arrogant self-confidence does not go with golf.

But this appreciation of the difficulty of mastering the game can influence a man too greatly. According to his interviewer, Dutra says that he has suffered from what he calls an inferiority complex. Although he must have known that he was a player of exceptional ability, still his unfailing good sense and his honesty with himself told him that he still could miss shots and throw away strokes—errors which he did not ascribe to the highly publicized stars against whom he was competing. He says that if he made a good shot he could always picture someone else making a better one. The infallibility which he awarded to others placed a burden upon his own game which it was not able to stand.

It is difficult for a person who has not been mixed up in these things to understand what it means to play a competitive round against opponents who cannot be seen. In an open championship one's imagination runs riot. A burst of applause or a cheer from a distant part of the course is always interpreted as a blow from some close pursuer, when it may mean no more than that some obscure competitor has holed a chip shot while another player's waiting gallery happened to be watching. It may not mean a thing, and even if it does, it can't be helped. But it is difficult to view it that way. One always feels that he is running from something without knowing exactly what nor where it is.

I used to feel just as Dutra did—that while I might make mistakes, that others would not. I remember looking at the scoreboard before the last round in the 1920 Open and deciding that I must do a 69 at the most to have a chance. Actually a 73 would have tied. I had some such lesson every year until I finally decided that the best of them made mistakes just as I did.

The advice which Harry Vardon is supposed to have given to keep on hitting the ball, no matter what happens, is the best in the long run. It is useless to attempt to guess what someone else will do, and worse than useless to set a score for yourself to shoot at. A brilliant round or a string of birdies will not always win a championship. The man who can put together four good rounds is the man to watch.

No man can expect to win at every start. Golf is not a game where such a thing is possible. So the plan should be to play one's own game as well as possible and let the rumors and cheers fly as thick as they will.

AFTERWORD

Half a million words. That's how many Bob Jones reckoned he wrote and published in the zenith of his championship golf career. Half a million. Each word carefully parsed, studied from all sides, and dropped into a sentence, like the cold finality of dropping a three-foot putt. He had plenty to write about. Like the half a million tears Jones likely shed during the Seven Lean Years journey across the desert of championships lost. And the half a million cheers which punctuated the most triumphant journey ever made in sports during the Seven Fat Ones. While in the desert, Jones confronted almost every conceivable way to lose. He suffered from his own sins and was sinned against. All the while Jones stockpiled half a million memories of ghost holes, self-imposed penalties, mercurial temper tantrums, concentration-robbing bumblebees, impetuous withdrawal from competition, and opponents blessed by "visitations" from God.

These were more than offset by half a million lessons in the best that life could offer Jones during his heyday years. On multiple occasions, Jones was the "dogged victim of inexorable fate," "struck down by appalling strokes of tragedy," became the "hero of unbelievable melodrama," and "the clown in many a side-splitting comedy."

Jones was especially able to write about the game. He once remarked that no golfer was especially suited to be a golf course architect just because he played well. In the same way, no golfer is specially suited to write about the game simply because he tasted victory. That is why most champions gladly defer to ghostwriters who separate the wheat from the chaff for them and put the best on paper. These "author" champions, quipped Charles Price, "had as much to do with the actual writing of them as King James did with writing the Holy Bible." On the other hand, there are no ghosts inside the dust jackets of Bob Jones' books.

Jones was able to write his own stuff because, of all the greatest champions in golf history, Jones was the best educated and possessed the most brilliant intellect. His analytical lawyer's mind was enriched by degrees from Georgia Tech in Mechanical Engineering and from Harvard in English Literature. Jones had both the practical and theoretical dimensions covered. His exceptional skills enabled him to carry on engaging conversations with kings and caddies alike.

This uncommon talent was showcased in Bob's first book, *Down the Fairway,* written in 1927 together with his best friend and fellow literary genius, O.B. Keeler. Once this cat was out of the bag, Jones was inundated with offers from various publishers. In those days an amateur was expressly permitted by USGA rules to be paid for writing books and articles without jeopardizing their amateur status. This was done in the name of educating the unwashed masses. Films were treated differently than the printed word, however, and anyone paid for acting in films was then deemed to forfeit his amateur status. The rationale for disparate treatment of these media was blurry at best and the risk was great. So Jones went out of his way to get an advance advisory USGA ruling when Jack Wheeler's Bell Syndicate made an acceptable offer in 1927. Bell Syndicate wanted Jones to write biweekly columns published in America and Great Britain. From 1927 until 1935, he wrote under the column headings "Bobby Jones Says," "My Theories of Golf," and "Bobby Jones on Golf."

It was astonishing stuff coming straight from the horse's mouth. Always before, O.B. Keeler was placed like a Chinese wall between Jones and the media. Jones never hung around the locker room drinking with the media and shooting the breeze. Instead, he returned to the inner sanctum of his hotel or a private home and the only stories about Jones' thoughts and ruminations were filtered through his biographer O.B. Keeler and regurgitated out to the masses like a terribly refined press release. It must have been awfully frustrating for the best writers never to get an exclusive from the greatest player ever. When Jones started his series, at least it was given firsthand.

Jones' personalized conversational style was immediately attractive and drew loyal audiences. The reader was finally able to glimpse into the window of the champion's mind. For instance, he wrote his thoughts immediately upon successfully defending his British Open title at St. Andrews:

> Last week in discussing the great difficulties for an American-bred player of British seaside golf and likewise in extolling the charm of playing overseas, I had constantly before my mind the Old Course at St. Andrews. In my humble opinion, it is the most fascinating golf course I have ever played; and if Pine Valley is as Chubby Hooman so delightfully expressed it, an examination, St. Andrews is a post-graduate course.

The pleasing diary style Jones employed in these early writings captured for posterity not only his experiences as a player, but also, his up close observation of the greatest players in the game.

Only hours after collecting his second victory toward the Grand Slam in 1930, Jones wrote in his Hoylake hotel room:

> This story tonight is by far the hardest one I have ever had to write.

* * *

> One great worry today was that even after I had suffered no end scrapping through my own round I had

to sit in the clubhouse while Compston Diegel and Mac Smith were playing the last nine holes. I felt very much as I know the defendant in a murder trial must feel as he waits for the jury to come in.

Jones' biweekly articles were a smash hit with his readers. They wrote letters back to him seeking more. And Jones did not disappoint his followers. He followed these initial articles with twelve one-reel films for Warner Brothers entitled, "How I Play Golf." Jones wrote all the technical stuff while O.B. Keeler filled in the story lines for the Hollywood actors and actresses who volunteered their time just to be on the same stage with Jones.

Using dictation, a tape recorder, and old-fashioned long-hand, Jones struggled with the manuscript. Sometimes Grant-land Rice "borrowed" the Bell Syndicate articles and "re-worked" them into a piece for the *American Golfer*. Jones recalled "in some cases there were some differences between Rice's published result and my convictions on the matter in question, but I never thought they were serious enough to worry too much about."

Thirty years later Jones observed that his theories were not only probably correct but also had been "innocently pla-giarized or even pirated" by those who followed him:

Nothing in my continuing observations of the great players has caused me to alter my convictions, and it does appear significant that even today I find coming back to me in spoken words, and from the printed page phrases I wrote more than thirty years ago. I mention this not at all as a complaint because I am pleased to have confirmation of my views from the ex-pert players and writers of today. The important as-pect, of course, is the proof then offered that the me-chanics of the effective golfing method are generally understood today to be the same as ever. Superficial conditions may have changed somewhat, but the fundamentals remain unaltered.

In the 1960s, Jones was approached by Charles Price to write his autobiography. He politely turned down the offer of five figures predicated on his rule against ghostwriters. Later, however, Jones agreed to help on another project. It was a book titled *Bobby Jones on Golf* based on the old Bell Syndicate articles. Together Price and Jones "skimmed the cream" off the top while selecting only about one-fifth of the total words for the end product. Price admitted "since all of these columns were unfailingly articulate what I tried to save from each was the timeless." When Charlie was through with what he thought was a masterpiece, "Jones then took the manuscript and, over a period of months, picked apart every chapter, every paragraph, every sentence, every phrase of his own writing until he was sure that thirty years had not dimmed what he had truly meant to say." It took a year and a half.

Jones' sense of humor about the project was never far from the surface. In one letter to Price, Jones remarked tongue-in-cheek:

> Your suggestion that we "pour" over the material for an hour or two puzzles me somewhat. We cannot do that here in the office you know.

Standing back to get a proper perspective of their labors, Price announced, "There wasn't a bromide in it."

The general reviews of the book by the golfing public and press were every bit as favorable as when the ideas were first penned. Jones noted "The book seems to have gotten some fairly good reviews except for Alister Cooke's which was excellent." *Bobby Jones on Golf* rang the cash register to the tune of 25,000 copies.

Jones' notoriety as a brilliant scribe put him in great demand for writing forewords and introductions to all kinds of golf books. If people couldn't see Bobby Jones play golf, at least they could stay connected by reading his stuff. Jones revealed much about golf and himself in no less than 15 forewords and introductions penned over the years. We learned that Horton Smith's "secret of holing putts" was because he "bore with a gimlet, not with an auger." No longer did one have to speculate why Gene Sarazen "lasted longer as a player than anyone of us who were at or near the top during the twenties." Jones' explanation of this seeming "agelessness" was simply a "success story of a hardheaded little guy who, throughout his life, has appraised with complete realism the adequacy of the tools he possessed for the accomplishment of purposes he saw very clearly." Jones' insight and humor were penetrating. As to Sarazen, Jones observed that his "articulations are usually printable, a quality not universally attributed to utterances of golfers as a class." In writing for Alister MacKenzie's "Lost Manuscript," Jones urged that all golfers should "know a good hole from a bad one and the reasons for a bunker here and another there, and he will be a long way towards pulling his score down to respectable limits." Only then Jones noted, "When he has taught himself to study a hole from the point of view of the man who laid it out, he will be much more likely to play it correctly." Because Jones was such a superb judge of character, he was able to pierce MacKenzie's very soul. In the foreword to O.B. Keeler's book, *The Bobby Jones' Story*, Jones described Keeler as an "understanding soul" who understood the "ebb and flow of a player's confidence" as one of the "strange phenomena of competitive golf." Not only did Keeler bolster Jones' confidence on the course, but what measure of fame Jones achieved "because of his proficiency in the inconsequential performance of striking a golf ball" was due in large part to Keeler and his "gifted typewriter." Although Jones disliked comparing golfers of different eras with watered-down superlatives, he found it "completely safe to say that there has not yet been a more effective golfer than Jack Nicklaus." After all, if Jones himself possessed "Jack's enormous power," then he could "think of nothing I should have enjoyed more than ripping into a tee shot with all of Jack's power." Nor was two-time Open champion Ralph Guldahl simply a player who "made great splurges in a season with natural ability not fortified with real understanding." Rather, he appreciated that the "first aim of form is simplicity." Glenna Collett, Johnny Farrell, Grantland Rice, J. Victor East, and Paul Runyan wrote books whose success was virtually assured by the inclusion of a Jones' foreword or introduction. How else would the reader discover the true essence of golf as "the most human of games" and a "reflection of life"? Lest we forget, Jones reminded us "the one saving grace is that we soon forget our disappointments and learn to remember and to laugh at our own foolishness" since golf is, after all, just a game.

The corpus of the original Bell Syndicate articles were never republished even though they too were well received. At Jones' death in 1971 *Newsweek* confirmed the "series of instructional articles are still widely recognized as the finest ever produced."

Sixty years later, respected golf journalists still marvel at the "spellbinding quality of Jones writing and oratory." Jerry Tarde, editor of *Golf Digest*, recently extolled the virtues of Jones' prose: "The simplicity of his revelations fell like thunderclaps across the page." Not unlike fine wine, Jones' golf writings have just gotten better and more appreciated with age.

Whereas, *Bobby Jones on Golf* skimmed the cream off the top, this work seeks to employ the whole milk too. Essentially, what was taken out of the original text by Jones and Price were many of the interesting stories and anecdotes that happened to Jones on his way to formulating the lessons at hand. While perhaps not "timeless," these chatty asides help to put some humor and humanity back into the mostly serious business of golf fundamentals. These stories also do much to help us appreciate just how Jones became inspired to write about these fundamentals in the first place. After all, these "conceptions" which Jones "set out are derived only from [his] experience in playing golf." That "experience" was only the most extraordinary in the history of the game.

As an eyewitness, Jones was particularly suited to testify to these stories on a first-hand basis:

> The best putting strokes I saw at Fresh Meadow were those employed by Sarazen and Perkins. The greens were fast and true, just the kind which reward a fine stroke. The characteristic of both was smoothness.

* * *

> Walter Hagen was playing fine golf up to the greens, but once there he had his troubles. I saw him miss a putt of not more than fifteen inches on the eighteenth green. Literally he jumped at the ball.

* * *

> Tommy Armour had most of his trouble off the tee. A heavier club might have slowed his swing down and helped his timing. There is nothing much worse than a fast back swing and snatchy hitting.

Later Jones wrote:

> I watched Francis Ouimet win the Massachusetts Open at Oyster Harbors . . . particularly there is a noticeable improvement in [Ouimet's] driving swing—the old tendency to lock the left hip having entirely disappeared.

In describing the difficulty of an approach from rough grass only a few feet of the putting surface, Jones commented:

> I think Harry Vardon was the most complete master of this stroke that I have seen. And Vardon always played

136

it in the gentlest way imaginable, in contrast to the quick, jerky, stroke employed by the average duffer. The long grass was seen as an added difficulty, but not one to be overcome by a hacking stroke.

Finally, on the subject of playing your own game and ignoring your opponent, Jones focused on psychology of golf:

> I remember looking at the scoreboard before the last round in the 1920 Open and deciding that I must do a 69 at the most to have a chance. Actually a 73 would have tied. I had some such lesson every year until I finally decided that the best of them made mistakes just as I did . . . It is useless to attempt to guess what someone else will do, and worse than useless to set a score for yourself to shoot at . . . So the plan should be to play one's own game as well as possible and let the rumors and cheers fly as thick as they will.

Some may say that "old-timers" like Jones don't have anything to offer the modern golfer. They might even argue that today's high-speed photography has rendered obsolete most of his theories. They would only be half right. And then they would have to turn back to Jones to learn the other half of the story:

> Our notion of the golf swing has changed much in the past thirty years. Principally by the aid of improved photography, both motion picture and the still ultra speed exposure, we have been able to learn much—to obtain demonstration of things we could only guess at before, and to disprove certain ideas we could arrive at only by feel. But the analytical exposition of the golf swing when it is slowed down or stopped for examination reveals nothing of rhythm or timing. For these we

must go to an actual observation of the swing itself or to the player himself to tell us the beat he swings in.

* * *

Rhythm and timing are the two things which we must all have, yet no one knows how to teach either.

* * *

The difficulty comes when we try to translate the actions of the picture into terms of muscular sense which will have a meaning for a person who has not experienced them. Anyone may observe the successive positions of these films. But to describe these positions in terms of "feel" which can enable a person who cannot see himself to execute the same motions is the job of the instructor.

Jones realized that you might get the right idea from modern imagery. But if you want to know about rhythm and timing and feel, you'll have to go to a knowledgeable player who knows how to explain it.

History has not revealed to us any more articulate person to explain this than Bobby Jones. For some it was enough for Jones to say simply "No one ever swung the club too slowly." But, for others, consider how Jones viewed "rhythm:"

We hear "slow back" on every side, but "slow back" is not enough. There are numbers of players who are able to restrain their impulses to this extent, but, who, once back, literally pounce on the ball with uncontrolled fury. It is the leisurely start downward which provides for a gradual increase of speed without disturbing the balance and timing of the swing.

* * *

Strive for rhythm. Let the backswing and the start downward be leisurely. I like this term better than "slow" because a swing might be too painfully slow. And always remember that there is plenty of space and time to gather speed between the top of the swing and the ball.

* * *

The only one who has a chance to achieve a rhythmic, well-timed stroke is the man who in spite of all else yet "swings his clubhead."

In conveying the mysteries of "feel," Jones masterfully shares his secrets gleaned from experience:

- "swing the clubhead"
- "fight tautness wherever it may make its appearance"
- "strive for relaxed muscles throughout"
- "simply turn during the backswing"
- "breakup whatever tension may exist and set the swing in easy motion"
- "promote the relaxed state"
- "stay down to the shot"
- "swing—don't hit"
- "the golfer's body is like a waving plume"
- "forward shift of the hips"
- "while the left leg straightens and stretches, it never braces itself"
- "left leg builds a 'column support' for the left shoulder"

- "head lifting itself results from a mechanical fault and does not itself start the trouble"

With myriad expressions at his command, Jones shares his secrets with us. Not because he particularly longs to write books, but rather because Jones genuinely enjoys doing his part to help everyone enjoy the game he loved so much:

There is no reason in the world why a competent instructor could not in a few short lessons instruct a pupil in a number of fundamentals which would help him play better and give him more pleasure without making the thing a drudgery for him. If he has no desire to go beyond that let him go on and play with his friends.

With Jones, everything is for the enjoyment of the game and the companionship of congenial friends. That is why these pages are so wonderfully informative and entertaining—today as well as when they were first written. This is especially true where, as here, Jones reveals to us the secrets of the master.

Sidney L. Matthew
Tallahassee